THE
UNITED STATES
IN THE
SPANISH-AMERICAN
WAR

THE UNITED STATES IN THE SPANISH-AMERICAN WAR

Don Lawson

Illustrated with photographs, and maps by Robert F. McCullough

Abelard-Schuman
New York

Library of Congress Cataloging in Publication Data

Lawson, Don. The United States in the Spanish-American War.
(The Young people's history of America's wars series) Bibliog-
raphy: p. Includes index.
  SUMMARY: Describes the causes and the events of the
Spanish-American War and how it led to the involvement of the
United States in the Philippine Insurrection and the Boxer
Rebellion.
  1. United States—History—War of 1898—Juvenile literature.
[1. United States—History—War of 1898] I. McCullough, Rob-
ert F., 1929–
II. Title.
E717.L38 1976   973.8′9   75-34165
ISBN 0-200-00163-9

Manufactured in the United States of America

10 9 8 7 6 5 4 3 2 1

To the Gartners—and especially
to Lois, for whom I trust I have
done right by T. R.

—D. L.

Books by DON LAWSON

The Young People's History of America's Wars Series

THE COLONIAL WARS: Prelude to the American
Revolution   (ISBN: 0-200-71885-1)

THE AMERICAN REVOLUTION: America's First
War for Independence   (ISBN: 0-200-00131-0)

THE WAR OF 1812: America's Second War for
Independence   (ISBN: 0-200-71441-4)

THE UNITED STATES IN THE INDIAN WARS
                          (ISBN: 0-200-00158-2)

THE UNITED STATES IN THE SPANISH-
AMERICAN WAR   (ISBN: 0-200-00163-9)

THE UNITED STATES IN WORLD WAR I: The
Story of General John J. Pershing and the American Expeditionary Forces (ISBN: 0-200-71939-4)

THE UNITED STATES IN WORLD WAR II:
Crusade for World Freedom (ISBN: 0-200-71795-2)

THE UNITED STATES IN THE KOREAN WAR:
Defending Freedom's Frontier (ISBN: 0-200-71803-7)

Contents

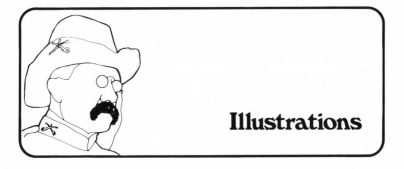

Illustrations

Time Line

1897

March 20—William McKinley takes office as twenty-fifth president of the United States.

1898

January 25—U.S. battleship *Maine* arrives in Havana harbor, Cuba, on a "friendly" visit.

February 15—Battleship *Maine* explodes from unknown cause, killing 260 crew members.

April 25—Congress declares state of war has existed between United States and Spain since April 21.

May 1—U.S. Commodore George Dewey destroys the Spanish fleet in Battle of Manila Bay in the Philippines.

June 14—U.S. Marines make their first landing on hostile soil in Spanish-American War at Guantanamo Bay, Cuba.

June 22–July 17—Battle of Santiago, Cuba; unable to use horses in this area, Colonel Theodore Roosevelt and his Rough Riders advance on foot.

July 1—Battle of El Caney, Cuba.

July 1–3—Battle of San Juan Hill and Kettle Hill, Cuba; Colonel Roosevelt's Rough Riders, Ninth and Tenth regiments of black troops, and a division of U.S. Regular Army infantry storm hills before Santiago, forcing Spaniards to break from their trenches and flee.

July 3—U.S. Navy destroys Spanish fleet at Santiago, Cuba.

July 7—Hawaiian Islands annexed by the United States.

July 31–August 14—Siege of Manila in the Philippines, ending in fall of Manila to U.S. forces; Dewey is unaware of war ending on August 12.

August 9–14—Porto Rico invaded and occupied by U.S. troops under General Nelson Miles.

August 12—United States signs preliminary peace agreement with Spain.

December 10—Official peace treaty signed at Paris between the United States and Spain; Cuba is freed; United States is ceded the Philippines, Guam and Porto Rico.

1899

February 4—Philippine Insurrection begins.

February 6—Senate ratifies Treaty of Paris by one-vote margin.

1900

June 20–August 15—U.S. troops from the Philippines take part in China Relief Expedition during the Boxer Rebellion.

1901

March 20—McKinley reinaugurated president of the United States; Roosevelt inaugurated as vice-president.

March 23—Emilio Aguinaldo, Filipino insurgent leader, captured.

September 14—McKinley dies from an assassin's bullet; Vice-President and former Rough Rider Theodore Roosevelt assumes office as the nation's youngest president.

1902

July 4—Philippine Insurrection officially ended by President Roosevelt's proclamation.

THE
UNITED STATES
IN THE
SPANISH-AMERICAN
WAR

"Remember the Maine!"

On January 25, 1898, the 24-gun United States battleship *Maine* anchored in Cuba's Havana harbor. The *Maine* was commanded by the U.S. Navy veteran, Charles D. Sigsbee, and had a crew of 350 officers and enlisted men.

Although there had been war clouds on the horizon for many months between the United States and Spain because of Spain's oppression of the Cuban people, the *Maine* had supposedly come to Cuba as a "friendly act of courtesy" to Spain. This warlike threat did not fool the Spanish, however. They promptly ordered an armored cruiser, the *Vizcaya*, to pay a "friendly visit" to New York.

Actually the *Maine* had been sent by President William McKinley to protect Americans and American property in Cuba after the American consul general there, Fitzhugh Lee, had reported a plot against U.S. citizens on the island.

1

The *Maine*'s captain and crew were greeted warmly enough by the Spanish in Havana. Captain Sigsbee was given gifts by the port commander, and Sigsbee, his officers and enlisted men were lavishly entertained ashore. Since there seemed to be no evidence of an anti-American plot nor any anti-American demonstrations, Navy Secretary John D. Long was about to recall the *Maine*. But Consul General Lee insisted that the battleship remain. At this point an unfortunate diplomatic incident occurred.

In Washington, the Spanish foreign minister to the United States, Dupuy de Lome, wrote a letter that was highly critical of President McKinley to a friend in Havana, José Canalejas. In the letter de Lome accused McKinley of being "weak and catering to the rabble" in his attitudes toward Spain. He also accused McKinley, among other things, of being a "low, coarse politician." Somehow this letter was stolen and turned over to an American newspaperman. The next day it was featured on the front pages of newspapers across the United States. It received special attention in the New York *Journal*, a paper owned by William Randolph Hearst, who had been loudly demanding war with Spain for some time because of its oppression of Cubans in their struggle for independence.

The Spanish foreign minister in Washington immediately cabled his resignation to Madrid, but the newspapers would not let the matter rest, despite the fact that even President McKinley could not see going to war with Spain over what amounted to a rather silly diplomatic blunder.

Nevertheless, the incident would probably have been gradually forgotten if an event that was far more serious and tragic had not occurred shortly afterwards.

The evening of February 15, 1898, was hot and humid in Havana. In the harbor aboard the *Maine* those members of the crew who had not gone ashore were sitting on deck or lying in their bunks belowdecks by open portholes, trying to take advantage of what little breeze was stirring. Some were writing letters home. Included among the latter was Captain Sigsbee, who was in his cabin writing a letter to his wife.

The melancholy bugle call of taps sounded across peaceful Havana harbor.

Then, suddenly, at precisely 9:40 P.M., the *Maine* erupted in an enormous explosion.

Captain Sigsbee was unhurt, but 260 of his crew died around him, either from the effects of the explosion or from drowning. Many men were saved by the crews of American small boats, and others were saved by the crew of a Spanish cruiser, the *Alfonso*. As a matter of fact, the Spaniards were as heroic as the Americans in their rescue efforts, despite the dangers from small arms ammunition, which was now going off like fireworks all around them, due to the major explosion.

Nevertheless, it would be the Spanish whom Americans would blame for blowing up the *Maine*. Hearst

U.S. battleship Maine *before sinking (inset shows the* Maine's *commander, Captain Charles D. Sigsbee).*

Wreck of the U.S. battleship **Maine** *blown up in Havana harbor.*

PHOTO: U.S. SIGNAL CORPS.

immediately announced exultantly, "This means war!" Joseph Pulitzer's newspaper, the *World*, left little doubt that the "accident" had been caused by enemy treachery. And across the land other newspapers and their readers took up the happy war cry:

Remember the Maine!
To hell with Spain!

Actually, it has not been decided to this day who was responsible for blowing up the *Maine*. Both the United States and Spain conducted official investigations. The U.S. naval court's conclusion was that "the *Maine* was destroyed by the explosion of a submarine [underwater] mine, which caused the partial explosion of two or more of the forward magazines." The court could fix no blame for the explosion. The Spanish inquiry resulted in a finding that indicated an accidental explosion inside the *Maine*. It too placed no blame, and guilt for the tragedy that triggered the Spanish-American War remains a mystery.

The events leading to this tragic occurrence in Havana harbor had begun in 1895, when an insurrection broke out on the island of Cuba with the Cuban people fighting for independence from their Spanish rulers. Most Americans were sympathetic with the Cubans, since their struggle against oppression was similar to America's early struggle for freedom from Great Britain. The United States, however, maintained an attitude of strict neutrality.

Then, in January 1896, Spain sent General Valeriano Weyler to Cuba with orders to deal harshly with the rebels. Weyler introduced what was called the reconcentration system. Under this system, men, women and children were herded into concentration camps that were not unlike those Adolf Hitler would introduce into Europe in World War II. Weyler's camps were overcrowded and undersupplied. Suffering from hunger and disease, the people in the camps died by the thousands.

The plight of the people in the reconcentration camps was played up in American newspapers, and especially in those newspapers owned by William Randolph Hearst and Joseph Pulitzer. Hearst's *Journal* and Pulitzer's *World* were carrying on a ruthless circulation war, and each competed with the other for bloodthirsty news out of Cuba, which seemed to appeal to American readers. Hearst was so determined on war with Spain that he had already sent the famous artist, Frederic Remington, to Havana to be there when hostilities began. When Remington became bored with the inactivity and cabled Hearst that he wanted to return to the United States, Hearst cabled back: "Please remain. You furnish the pictures and I'll furnish the war."

This warmongering newspaper campaign further inflamed public opinion by referring to General Weyler as "Butcher" Weyler and always picturing the Cuban insurgents—many of whom had resorted to murder, assassination and other terroristic methods in their rebellion—as high-minded patriots cut from the same cloth as the American freedom fighters of 1776. In addition, numerous American politicians attempted to ride the wave of popular public opinion by denouncing Spain. Others saw this crisis in the Caribbean as a bright opportunity to gain outposts and naval bases that would lead to a bigger role for the United States in world power and politics.

While Grover Cleveland was president, demands for U.S. intervention gained little ground. William McKinley also claimed to be opposed to war, but he allowed himself to be pushed into it by the course of events. The first of these events was the Dupuy de Lome letter insulting McKinley, which the newspapers and reading public reacted to as a national insult. The second was the sinking of the *Maine*.

McKinley made a few weak efforts to combat the storm of public emotion that swept the nation following the *Maine* disaster. On March 27 a letter that amounted to an ultimatum was sent to Spain demanding the abolishment of all reconcentration camps, an amnesty for all Cuban insurgents and the right of the United States to act as an arbitrator between the rebels and Spain.

Spain seemed willing to go along with this ultimatum, although instant agreement probably would have resulted in the overthrow of the Spanish monarchy. But even momentary delay was too much for the U.S. Congress. On April 19 it proclaimed Cuba independent and authorized McKinley to use land and sea forces to expel Spain from Cuba. McKinley signed the

William Randolph Hearst.

congressional joint resolution the next day and, on April 25, Congress declared that a state of war had existed between the United States and Spain since April 21. Hearst's *Journal* headlined the declaration with:

NOW TO AVENGE THE MAINE!

And so began what one U.S. statesman, Ambassador to England John Hay, was later to call "A splendid little war," and another U.S. statesman and combat hero, Theodore Roosevelt, was to describe as, "Not much of a war but the only one we had." However, historians have long since agreed that it was a completely unnecessary war, caused largely by a weak and irresolute president, warmongering newspapers and a misguided American public that thought it was embarked on a combination crusade and "picnic." This would prove to be a tragic error in judgment.

"You May Fire When Ready, Gridley!"

When the United States declared war on Spain, the U.S. Regular Army numbered some 28,000 men who were stationed at numerous posts throughout the country. Congress at once voted to double the size of the regular army. It also authorized a call for, first, 125,000, and then 267,000 volunteers. Drafting men into military service was not considered because no draft was necessary. More than a million men immediately volunteered for this Caribbean "picnic" that the whole nation seemed to want to attend.

But the volunteers found anything but picnic conditions once they got into their camps. Their officers were untrained; there was a severe shortage of equipment and supplies; sanitary conditions were poor; food was bad or nonexistent; there was inadequate medical service and what there was was poor and weapons and ammunition were obsolete at best.

President McKinley signing the ultimatum to Spain.

Uniforms were made of heavy wool even though the training camps were mainly in the south and the campaign would be in the tropics. It was not many weeks before volunteer troops became bored from lack of activity, sick and filled with despair.

The truth of the matter was that the regular army was almost totally unprepared for war. Many of its officers were aging veterans of the Civil War and the Indian Wars, and the army high command had neither mobilization plans nor any experience or plans for that most difficult of all military operations—an amphibious assault. The high command had no knowledge whatsoever of Spanish troop strength or the exact location of troops in either Cuba or the Philippines, both of which would have to be invaded. Finally, there was no plan at all for military operations once American troops had gone ashore.

The National Guard numbered about 100,000 men whose training consisted mainly of close-order drill and marching. Their military knowledge was at raw-recruit level, and their few weapons were obsolete. To compound the confusion, each state had its own rules regarding its own National Guard. So there were as many guard armies as there were states, and none wanted to be under control of the regular army.

Major General Nelson A. Miles, veteran of the Civil War and the Indian Wars, was commanding general of the United States Army. He ordered that the whole regular army be trained together at Chickamauga Park, Georgia. But the secretary of war, Russell

Lieutenant General Nelson A. Miles. A veteran of both the Indian and Civil wars, Miles was kept in Washington during most of the Spanish-American War. He did manage to lead campaign against Porto Rico but never became a popular hero. He had hoped his role in the war would lead to the presidency. Miles's postwar charges against the War Department's mismanagement of supplying edible food to troops in the field caused a national scandal and led in time to investigation of the entire meat-packing industry.

PHOTO: U.S. SIGNAL CORPS.

A. Alger, heartily disliked Miles. Alger countermanded Miles's orders, and directed the cavalry and artillery to train at Chickamauga and the infantry to move to New Orleans, Louisiana; Tampa, Florida; and Mobile, Alabama, and prepare to set sail for Cuba just as soon as troop transports were available. The only additional problem was that there were no transports available and none would soon be forthcoming because the army owned not a single troopship. In time, 38 were chartered from private owners. But in the end most of the several hundred thousand troops that were in service during the few months of the war never left the United States.

Fortunately for the United States, the Spanish were in an equally bad, if not worse, state of military preparedness. The Spanish had 200,000 troops in Cuba, but no more than half of these ever took part in the conflict. Those that did see combat were poorly supplied, and the attacks in which they took part were poorly planned and badly executed. Cuban troops played no truly decisive role in deciding the war's outcome.

Also, fortunately for the United States, the U.S. Navy was far better prepared for the conflict than the army. Most Europeans thought the Spanish navy, which numbered 137 ships, would easily defeat the American navy, but they were wholly unaware of the new steel fleet that the United States had created on the eve of the war. Even so, many service and supply ships had to be refitted and rearmed to be converted into warships. At the outbreak of war the United States had 69 warships, including four 10,000-ton first-class battleships. Within a few months 67 more warships were acquired, bringing the total to 136. The number of men manning the fleet was quickly increased from 14,000 to more than 24,000.

There were two men directly responsible for the preparedness of the U.S. Navy at the outbreak of the Spanish-American War. The first was an authority on seapower, Captain (later Admiral) Alfred T. Mahan. The second was a public official and active participant in both preparing for and fighting the war, Theodore Roosevelt.

Mahan, a graduate of the Naval Academy, had served at sea during the Civil War. After that war, he became president of the Naval Academy, where he wrote his great work, *The Influence of Seapower Upon History*. In this book Mahan pointed out the importance of the control of the seas of the world to a nation's prosperity and power in both peace and war. He illustrated his theory of success through seapower by pointing out that virtually every leading nation throughout history had been a leading nation because it had controlled the sea-lanes to and from its shores.

"In the past," Mahan wrote, "those nations which have made intelligent use of seapower have prospered greatly, whereas the reverse is true of those who failed to comprehend its use and importance." He also quoted the Athenian statesman, Themistocles, who said, "Whosoever can hold the sea has command of the

Admiral Alfred T. Mahan. He took no active part in the war, but his book on the importance of seapower influenced the war's outcome.

PHOTO: U.S. BUREAU OF SHIPS.

situation." And 2,000 years later, Mahan further observed, this opinion, held in common by ancient Greece and Rome, was reechoed by Sir Walter Raleigh, who stated, "Whosoever commands the trade of the world, commands the riches of the world and consequently the world itself."

Mahan's theory became popular almost at once and greatly influenced both military and public opinion in Europe and America. Great Britain and Germany were among the leading European nations to accept Mahan's seapower doctrine and began to build steel fleets. In the United States, steel ships had begun to replace wooden war vessels during the Civil War. During this "naval revolution," steam power replaced sail, armor was widely used on ships' hulls and rifled guns replaced smoothbore cannons. But, with the end of the Civil War, the navy was allowed to decline until Mahan's seapower theory reawakened U.S. naval leaders to the need for a completely new steel war fleet. The first of these new ships was authorized in 1883. It and the several that followed became the nucleus for the new navy, upon which Theodore Roosevelt was to build.

When William McKinley became president in 1897, he brought Roosevelt to Washington as assistant secretary of the navy. Roosevelt—affectionately known as Teddy or T. R.—had served the federal government previously, as the civil service commissioner. Before that he had served in the New York State legislature as its youngest assemblyman, and later he became New York City's fearless police commissioner. But it was the

18

Spanish-American War that was to make Teddy Roosevelt a nationally known figure. Eventually the fame he gained in that war would lead to his becoming vice-president of the United States and then president, following McKinley's assassination by Leon Czolgosz in 1901.

Although Roosevelt was an aggressive and courageous man, both mentally and physically, he had not come by those traits easily. Born on October 27, 1858, he was a sickly child suffering from asthma. When he was still a youngster, however, his father had a gymnasium built in the family home where young Teddy could work out. Daily, for hours at a time, the boy exercised in the gym. He also learned to box and became quite skilled at the sport. At Harvard University, from which he graduated in 1880, young Roosevelt was both an outstanding athlete and a scholar, winning a boxing championship in his junior year and being elected to Phi Beta Kappa when he was a senior.

Roosevelt also knew tragedy early in his life. A few months after his graduation from Harvard he married Alice Lee, his college sweetheart. Teddy's father had died at the age of forty-six, so Teddy, his wife and his widowed mother lived together in New York City where Teddy was studying law and beginning to take an interest in politics. There, early in 1884, his wife and mother died in the same house and on the same day, February 14. His wife died shortly after giving birth to a daughter, Alice, and the elder Mrs. Roosevelt died of typhoid fever.

After his tragic loss, Roosevelt buried his grief in

Teddy Roosevelt in boxing outfit at Harvard.
PHOTO: THEODORE ROOSEVELT ASSOCIATION.

the hard work of managing a cattle ranch in the Bad Lands of North Dakota, leaving the baby, Alice, in the care of his older sister. Roosevelt invested a considerable amount of the family money he had inherited in the ranching venture, most of which he lost when his cattle were wiped out in severe blizzards. Despite his financial losses in the Bad Lands, Roosevelt never lost his love of the West, where he felt he had truly learned the value of what he was fond of calling "the strenuous life." Nor did he forget the friends he made there among the cowboys—and the cowboys never forgot him. They were to ride and fight their way to fame and glory together in Cuba during the Spanish-American War.

Roosevelt returned to New York in 1886 and reentered politics, making an unsuccessful bid for mayor. He also remarried, this time to a childhood friend, Edith Kermit Carow. They had five children, Theodore, Jr., Kermit, Ethel, Archibald and Quentin. The huge, rambling house in which the colorful Teddy Roosevelt family lived at Oyster Bay, Long Island, became nationally famous as Sagamore Hill.

When Benjamin Harrison ran for president in 1888, Teddy Roosevelt campaigned for him. When Harrison was elected, he named Roosevelt civil service commissioner. In this role Roosevelt instituted numerous civil service reforms that are still in effect. Grover Cleveland, Harrison's successor to the presidency, thought so highly of Roosevelt's efforts that he kept him on in the civil service job. Then, in 1894,

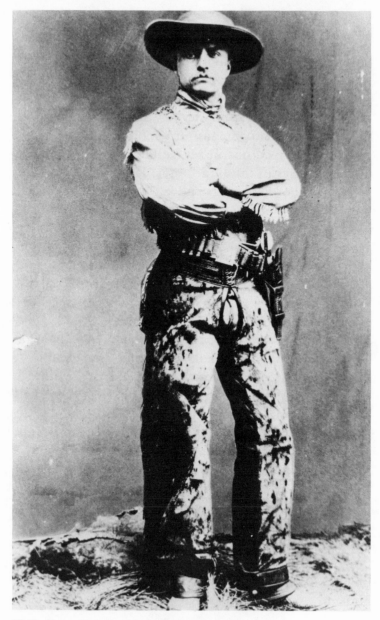

Teddy Roosevelt during his days as a cowboy.

PHOTO: THEODORE ROOSEVELT ASSOCIATION.

Roosevelt accepted the appointment as New York City's police commissioner. Soon he had rid the city, as well as the police department, of much of the graft, corruption, and favoritism with which it had been afflicted. It was from this post that President McKinley had called him to Washington to become assistant secretary of the navy.

McKinley had known that Roosevelt was honest, headstrong, fearless and bluntly outspoken—too outspoken, many said—but he hadn't really seen him in action. When he did, the mild-mannered McKinley said, "I'm afraid our Teddy acts a little bit too much like a bull in a china shop."

But now Teddy Roosevelt was too busy "getting a job of work done," as he put it, to pay attention to anyone, let alone the president of the United States. Teddy saw war with Spain looming on the horizon, and he grew increasingly impatient with McKinley's attempts to avoid the conflict, even going so far as to accuse the president of having "no more backbone than a chocolate eclair." When war came, Roosevelt meant for the U.S. Navy to be ready for it.

One of the things he did was to ramrod through Congress additional money appropriations for new warships. Secondly, he became intimately acquainted with the senior officers of all U.S. battleships, and the records of these officers from their first day of command. What Roosevelt was looking for were bold commanders who knew their profession, but did not stand on ceremony, and had been at battle stations

Admiral George Dewey aboard his flagship, Olympia. *Dewey overwhelmingly defeated Admiral Patricio Montojo aboard the* Reina Cristina *as well as the rest of the Spanish fleet at Manila in the first major engagement of the war.*

when the first shots were fired in anger. One such man he found in Commodore George Dewey, a naval hero of the Civil War. Also a graduate of the Naval Academy, Dewey had served as executive officer aboard the U.S.S. *Mississippi* in David Farragut's fleet and later served on Farragut's flagship. Farragut's motto, which Dewey quickly adopted, was: "Damn the torpedoes. Full steam ahead!" He was the kind of fleet commander Roosevelt was seeking.

Roosevelt placed Dewey in command of the U.S. Asiatic Squadron and told him to have the squadron ready for action in the Philippine Islands, if war broke out with Spain. Actually, almost everybody thought that war, if it came, would begin in Cuba. Not very many people were aware that Spain also owned the Philippines and had a part of its fleet stationed there. But Roosevelt knew it and acted on the knowledge. And, after the first major battle of the Spanish-American War was fought there, President McKinley said that he wasn't even sure where the Philippines were!

Immediately after the U.S. battleship *Maine* was sunk in Havana harbor, Roosevelt cabled Commodore Dewey:

KEEP SHIPS FULL OF COAL. IN THE EVENT OF A
DECLARATION OF WAR WITH SPAIN, YOUR DUTY WILL
BE TO SEE THAT THE SPANISH SQUADRON DOES NOT
LEAVE THE ASIATIC COAST. THEN BEGIN OFFENSIVE
OPERATIONS IN PHILIPPINE ISLANDS.

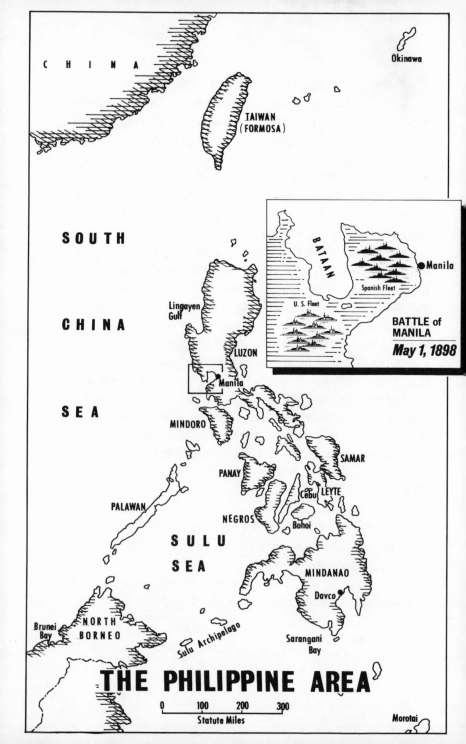

THE PHILIPPINE AREA

BATTLE of MANILA
May 1, 1898

0   100   200   300
Statute Miles

Early on Sunday morning, May 1, 1898, Commodore Dewey's squadron steamed into Manila Bay. Sighting the Spanish ships, Dewey said casually to the captain of the flagship *Olympia*, "You may fire when ready, Gridley." A few moments later the guns of the American fleet began to rain down death and destruction.

By midday every Spanish ship in Manila Bay was out of action. Ten of the enemy's major warships were sunk, and about 400 Spanish sailors were killed. Not a single American ship was badly damaged, and no American lives were lost. Less than a week after the declaration of war, the United States had its first major victory to celebrate.

The Rough Riders

Though Roosevelt was proud of Dewey's victory in Manila Bay and the role he had played in it, he was not content with remaining on the sidelines in Washington. He too wanted to take part in the action. Out of this desire grew the soon-to-be-famous Rough Riders.

One of the friends that Roosevelt made during his first months as assistant secretary of the navy was an army surgeon and White House physician named Leonard Wood. Wood had served with General Miles during the Indian Wars, where he had won the Congressional Medal of Honor for conspicuous bravery against the fierce Apaches. Although Wood was an excellent doctor, he preferred combat duty. Roosevelt and Wood immediately realized that they were kindred spirits. Roosevelt believed that war for a righteous cause brought out the finest virtues in both men and

Colonel Leonard Wood, commander of the Rough Riders and later military governor of Cuba.

PHOTO: U.S. SIGNAL CORPS.

nations, and Wood agreed with him. Wood also agreed when Roosevelt said, "No triumph of peace is quite so great as the supreme triumph of war."

When the *Maine* was sunk, both Roosevelt and Wood knew that war with Spain was inevitable. They immediately began to seek ways of getting into the fighting when war began. The president was opposed to their leaving their posts in Washington but said he would not stand in the way if they insisted upon going.

Wood decided he would try to get a commission in a volunteer unit from Massachusetts, his native state, but—as in every other state—there were ten volunteers for every military vacancy. Roosevelt experienced the same situation in trying for duty with the New York State volunteer regiments.

Their problem was solved when Congress authorized the raising of three cavalry regiments from the cowboys in the West and Southwest. During Wood's service against the Apaches in the Southwest, he had commanded both frontiersmen, who had acted as Indian scouts, and hard-riding, hard-fighting cowboys. And Roosevelt, of course, had spent much time at his ranch in the North Dakota Bad Lands living and working with cowboy ranch hands.

Secretary of War Alger offered Roosevelt the command of one of these three cavalry regiments. But Roosevelt had no military training and knew it would take him months just to learn the necessary administrative procedures. Wood, on the other hand, was an experienced military man and was the logical person to command the regiment. Roosevelt suggested to Alger that Wood be named the colonel in command. Both Alger and President McKinley agreed, and Wood was commissioned colonel and Roosevelt, as second in command, was commissioned lieutenant colonel of the First United States Volunteer Cavalry. As soon as the unit began to be formed, however, the newspapers began to refer to it as the "Rough Riders," and the public never called it anything else. Both Wood and Roosevelt fought against their regiment's nickname but, when the top army command referred to the Rough Riders in all official orders and military communications, Wood and Roosevelt adopted the nickname themselves.

Wood and Roosevelt's immediate problem was not in selecting but in rejecting men to serve with the Rough Riders. As soon as the announcement was made that such a regiment was to be raised, applications to join it arrived from every state in the Union. In addition, Roosevelt was besieged by old Harvard classmates, policemen who had served under him when he was New York City's police commissioner and ranch owners he had known in North Dakota. At first, Roosevelt thought he would have to turn down most of these volunteers but, when the size of the regiment was increased from 780 to 1,000 men, he was able to accept many of them, especially those who were outstanding athletes from Harvard and other Ivy League schools. In accepting them, Roosevelt made it clear that they would probably have to serve in the ranks as privates

Applicants for enlistment studying recruiting circulars in front of New York post office.

PHOTO: U.S. SIGNAL CORPS.

and do all of the hard, dull and menial tasks that are the common soldier's lot. No one was to expect special privileges because he was a college man. None did— then or later.

The bulk of the regiment, however, was made up of cowboys, Texas Rangers, hunters and mining prospectors from the West and Southwest. They went by such nicknames as "Tough Ike," "The Dude," "Metropolitan Bill," "Pork Chop," "Hell Roarer" and "Prayerful James." "They were a splendid set of men," Roosevelt said, "tall and sinewy, with resolute, weather-beaten faces, and eyes that looked a man straight in the face without flinching."

In addition, there were a number of Indians who volunteered just for the sheer adventure. These included Cherokees, Chickasaws, Choctaws and Creeks. Only a few years earlier the Indians' wars with the white man had ended, and now redman and white man would be fighting side by side.*

Wood and Roosevelt's next major problem was in obtaining weapons, ammunition, horses, uniforms, supplies and all the other necessary military equipment. With hundreds of regiments being raised, the competition for such needs was fierce. Knowing the army's state of unpreparedness for the war, Colonel Wood also knew that it would be months before the ordnance and quartermaster's departments would be able to meet all the demands placed upon them.

* See another book in this series, *The United States in the Indian Wars*.

Lieutenant Colonel Theodore Roosevelt, second in command, Rough Riders.

Consequently, it was essential to get the Rough Riders' demands in first. Wood did this and then proceeded to hound the various officials until the requests were filled. Within a matter of weeks, Wood had obtained all of the necessary rifles, revolvers, ammunition, clothing, tents and cavalry-horse equipment to outfit the regiment.

One of Wood's most important achievements was in obtaining the latest carbines plus an ample supply of smokeless gunpowder which had just recently been developed. As a result of Wood's efforts, the Rough Riders were ready to go into action long before any other volunteer regiments. Consequently, they were to see far more fighting than any other volunteers and most regulars.

The Rough Riders were assembled for training at San Antonio, Texas. Here Colonel Wood and other officers who had served with him in the Indian Wars began to instill discipline into their rookie soldiers from the Wild West. Many did not take too well to such niceties as saluting and speaking respectfully to officers. But Wood was rigid and inflexible in his demands on them. Nor did they appreciate drilling on foot when they were used to riding horses. Eventually such training was to prove invaluable, however, for when they got to Cuba they would find the terrain such that it was impossible to go into combat on horseback. Gradually, the men learned close- and open-order maneuvers, advancing in a line of skirmish-

Rough Riders' officers' mess at San Antonio.

PHOTO: U.S. SIGNAL CORPS.

ers, and firing their weapons on command. Most of the men had been using firearms all of their lives so they needed little training in hitting targets, but they did have to learn the necessary discipline of firing and cease-firing by direct orders.

When horses were purchased it was soon discovered that most had never been broken to the saddle. This delighted many of the cowboys, who liked nothing better than to hold impromptu bronco-riding contests. Mounted order drill on partially broken and wholly undisciplined horses often resulted in what more closely resembled a stampede than it did a cavalry charge. But eventually the men established their authority over their half-wild animals, and mounted drill in line and column formations began to go more smoothly.

The Rough Riders' uniforms suited their devil-may-care spirit. Roosevelt later wrote, "In their slouch hats, blue flannel shirts, brown trousers, leggings and boots, with handkerchiefs knotted loosely around their necks they looked exactly as a body of cowboy cavalry should look."

Just when both men and horses were rounding into shape, orders were received for the Rough Riders to proceed by train to Tampa, Florida, where they were to board transports bound for Cuba. The troop train carrying more than 1,000 officers and men, plus attached freight cars carrying more than 1,000 horses and 250 mules, moved out for Tampa on Sunday, May

29, 1898. They arrived four days later, hungry, thirsty, dirty, hot and exhausted from lack of sleep. But their spirits remained high. The great Cuban adventure was about to begin.

The Message to Garcia

Before any invasion of Cuba could be attempted, however, it was essential that the U.S. Navy locate a fleet of Spanish warships that had reportedly sailed for Cuba from Spain shortly before the war began. It was essential to find and destroy this fleet, commanded by Admiral Pasqual Cervera, not only to protect American troopships bound for Cuba but also to protect American cities along the eastern seaboard which the Spanish—so the rumor went—had threatened to attack.

Actually, Admiral Cervera had undertaken the voyage with great reluctance, and he had no intention of attacking American cities. He had regarded the outbreak of war as a tragedy and predicted "catastrophe for poor Spain and the Spanish fleet." When ordered to sail, he said, "Our voyage to America will be disastrous for the future of our country." The destruction of many of Spain's warships in Manila harbor in the Philippines was to fulfill part of Cervera's prophecy, and he himself was to be in charge of the prophecy's complete fulfillment with the destruction of the remainder of the Spanish fleet outside Cuba's Santiago Bay.

But American citizens in cities along the Atlantic seaboard went into a panic when the rumor reached them that they were about to be attacked by the Spanish raiders. Completely unreasonable demands for protection were made upon the U.S. Navy. In response to these demands, the navy created a Flying Squadron under the command of Commodore Winfield S. Schley that was charged with defending the east coast. In addition, ancient Civil War vessels called monitors were anchored in the harbors of coastal cities to prevent the entry of enemy warships, a role for which they were completely useless, but their presence was reassuring to alarmed citizens. The main body of the U.S. Atlantic fleet was assigned the task of blockading Cuban ports and destroying Cervera's fleet if it appeared in Caribbean waters. (Curiously, American citizens on the west coast were later to experience a similar mindless panic at the start of World War II, when it was feared that San Francisco and other coastal cities would be bombed by Japanese aircraft. Despite the fact that the Japanese had no bases from which to launch such aerial bombing attacks, fear of them resulted in nightly blackouts of all cities and numerous coastal alerts that resulted in more automobile accidents and casualties than there would have been in several full-scale air raids.)*

To strengthen the U.S. Atlantic fleet, the battleship *Oregon* had earlier been ordered to sail under a full head of steam from its station in the Pacific on a 12,000-mile journey around the southern tip of South America and into the Caribbean. (It was this emergency war maneuver that brought home to Theodore Roosevelt the great need for a shorter route between the Atlantic and Pacific oceans that later led to the building of the Panama Canal. The *Oregon*'s trip would have been only about 4,500 miles through such a canal.)

Most naval experts were certain that the *Oregon* would founder in the stormy Strait of Magellan, but Captain Charles E. Clark, who was then in command of the *Oregon*, brought his ship safely through some of the worst gales either he or his crew had ever experienced. And they made the journey in record time—68 days!

Panic among the citizens along the Atlantic coast grew as the whereabouts of Cervera and the Spanish fleet remained a mystery for several weeks. However, U.S. Admiral William T. Sampson, in charge of the Atlantic fleet, was not alarmed. The Spanish warships included four armored cruisers and two destroyers, and Sampson was certain Cervera would not risk his smaller vessels against the American battleships. In

* See another book in this series, *The United States in World War II*.

this Sampson proved correct. After skillfully eluding the American Atlantic fleet, Cervera sailed his warships safely into Cuba's Santiago Bay. But, in entering Santiago Bay, Cervera sealed his own fate. Sampson simply ordered that the Cuban port be blockaded and began a bombardment of the forts at the entrance to Santiago Bay.

To tighten the blockade and prevent Cervera's fleet from leaving the bay, Sampson decided to sink a large U.S. ship in the middle of the narrow entrance channel. The ship selected was a coal-carrying vessel (called a collier), the *Merrimac*, and the officer selected to take charge of the operation was Lieutenant Richard P. Hobson.

Fitting the *Merrimac* with ten torpedoes that could be exploded by remote battery control, Hobson and a crew of seven volunteers set off on their dangerous mission on a dark, moonless night. Hobson planned to anchor the *Merrimac* in the middle of the harbor entrance, open the ship's sea valves so it would be flooded and sink, escape the foundering craft in a small lifeboat and then explode the torpedoes.

But dark as it was, Spanish gunners in the port's fortresses spotted the *Merrimac* before it had reached the center of the channel and began to bombard it. Soon the vessel drifted off target and sank. Hobson and his crew were rescued and taken prisoners by Admiral Cervera himself, aided by crew members from the Spanish fleet. Cervera courteously informed Admiral Sampson of the outcome of the venture. Although the sunken *Merrimac* did not block the channel, Hobson and his men were hailed as heroes throughout the United States when the Hearst and Pulitzer newspapers told the story of their feat. Hobson was later decorated by the U.S. Navy.

Admiral Sampson now prepared for a lengthy siegelike blockade of Santiago Bay. To make certain he would have a permanent and safe base for refueling his ships with coal from other colliers like the *Merrimac*, Sampson ordered two ships, the *Marblehead* and the *Yankee*, under Commander B. H. McCalla, to capture nearby Guantanamo and gain control of Guantanamo's excellent harbor. Beginning on June 14, a force of some 750 marines under Lieutenant Colonel Robert W. Huntington were put ashore. At first, they encountered only light resistance and immediately began to establish a base there called Camp McCalla. Within a short time, however, the Spanish began to attack Camp McCalla in nightly raids. U.S. Marine counterattacks finally drove the enemy inland and out of effective combat range. These marines were the first U.S. troops to land on Cuban soil in the Spanish-American War, and Camp McCalla was the first U.S. military base established there. The Guantanamo Bay naval installation has remained in U.S. hands right up to the present day. Once again the Hearst and Pulitzer newspapers broke out their biggest, boldest type to announce:

THE MARINES HAVE LANDED!

One of the newspaper correspondents who accompanied this expedition was a young man named Stephen Crane, who had earlier written a famous novel about the Civil War, *The Red Badge of Courage*. Interestingly, Crane had never heard a shot fired in anger before the Spanish-American War, but he now discovered that combat was every bit as grim and bloody as he had so vividly imagined it in his novel.

The war proved to be almost as much of a newspaper correspondents', artists' and photographers' war as it was a military operation. In addition to Frederic Remington and Stephen Crane, the famous foreign correspondent, Richard Harding Davis, added to his already brilliant reputation—during his lifetime he was to cover six major wars—by accompanying front-line troops right into combat, even aiding Teddy Roosevelt in a later land battle by pointing out the enemy hidden in heavy saw grass. He was among the first newspapermen ever to be such an active participant in combat.

But the author of the most famous piece of writing to come out of the war never saw Cuba. This was Elbert Hubbard, a New York State publisher, philosopher and essayist. Hubbard's famous if somewhat fictionalized essay, "A Message to Garcia," was inspired by an actual incident that took place early in the war. It involved the Cuban rebel general, Calixto Garcia, and a young U.S. Army lieutenant, Andrew S. Rowan.

Garcia was a Cuban lawyer and the rebel general

Cuban General Calixto Garcia. A former lawyer, Garcia led Cuban rebels against the Spanish in the revolt of 1895–98, leading to the Spanish-American War.

who commanded the insurgent Cuban army in the revolution of 1895 to 1898 that immediately preceded the Spanish-American War. When the United States declared war against Spain, Garcia and 5,000 men besieged the Spanish garrison at Santiago before the American troops landed.

When hostilities between the United States and Spain began, General Nelson Miles sent Lieutenant Rowan into Cuba on his own to find Garcia and give him a message asking the specific kind of aid the United States should immediately send. Rowan, disguised as a British sportsman, was put ashore at night by a navy gunboat and immediately disappeared into the Cuban jungles. Although he had no knowledge regarding Garcia's whereabouts, Rowan moved bravely across the island to inquire directions, making use of the Spanish he had learned during previous army service in South America. Three weeks later Rowan stumbled into Garcia's headquarters with his message, and a short time later Garcia's needs were made known to General Miles by a triumphantly returning Lieutenant Rowan, who was escorted back to the coast by Garcia's rebel soldiers.

Elbert Hubbard wrote an inspirational essay based on Rowan's heroic, if blind, obedience to orders. Hubbard had always believed that all jobs worth doing were worth doing well, and Rowan's doing his job—faithfully carrying the message to Garcia—was the perfect illustration of this. Hubbard wrote the essay in an hour—a fact of which he was always proud—and it

Lieutenant Andrew S. Rowan. He carried the message to Garcia.

PHOTO: U.S. SIGNAL CORPS.

was an instant nationwide success because millions of copies were printed and sold across the land.

Lieutenant Rowan was now hailed as the war's brightest hero to date, although Roosevelt and his Rough Riders were soon to eclipse the glow of Rowan's star. It wasn't until 1920, however, 11 years after Rowan had retired, that the army finally recognized his exploit by awarding him the Distinguished Service Cross. Hubbard was to go on to even greater popularity as a writer, but was, ironically, to meet his death by drowning as a passenger aboard the *Lusitania*, the ocean liner the Germans torpedoed and sank off the coast of Ireland in 1915 early in World War I.

First Major Landings

Meanwhile, back in Tampa, the army was trying to organize its amphibious assault on Cuba. When they arrived in Tampa, not only the Rough Riders but also thousands of other troops—both volunteers and regulars—encountered a state of total confusion. And with each passing day matters seemed to grow worse.

Major General William R. Shafter was in overall command of the American Fifth (V) Corps assault forces. Shafter was a former Civil War officer with an excellent combat record. But since that conflict he had grown quite fat and now weighed about 300 pounds. Tampa's tropical heat as well as the chaotic conditions at the port of embarkation proved too much for the enormous Shafter. (Later, at the Battle of San Juan Hill, Shafter—along with another key U.S. general, Joseph Wheeler—was to be forced out of action because of the heat.)

General Joseph Wheeler, third from left, and Colonel Roosevelt, far right, at Tampa. Other officers are unidentified.

PHOTO: U.S. SIGNAL CORPS.

Actually, no worse place could have been chosen for the embarkation of the expedition. There was only one railroad track leading to the port's single pier. When it began, the embarkation was completely unorganized. There were no plans for the troop movement, and Shafter's staff was not on hand to coordinate the boarding of transports by the various units. Almost no attention was paid to the correct order of loading troops and their essential supplies for an amphibious assault. Men and war materiel were simply dumped aboard transports hit-or-miss, with no thought given to what supplies and equipment might be needed immediately after a landing was made. Some combat units simply took matters into their own hands, commandeering railroad cars to transport them to the pier and there engaging in fistfights to see who had the right to board the few available transports. Included among the outfits that took matters into their own hands were, of course, the Rough Riders.

Teddy Roosevelt was among the first to realize that if he and Colonel Wood did not move out their troops, nobody was going to do it for them. Since no troop trains were available, Roosevelt loaded the Rough Riders aboard a coal train and ordered the engineer to take them the nine miles to the port. When they arrived there a few hours later—covered with coal dust but with their personal belongings intact—no one knew what transport they or the 10,000 other troops, milling about the quay, were supposed to board.

After several more hours, Wood took command of

Port of embarkation at Tampa.

PHOTO: U.S. SIGNAL CORPS.

Embarkation of troops for Cuba.

PHOTO: U.S. SIGNAL CORPS.

There were a dozen of more navy warships and 32 transports in the convoy that carried about 16,000 men, most of whom had gone through the same ordeal

a motor launch and headed for a transport called the *Yucatan*. After Wood had boarded the *Yucatan* and ordered its captain to head for the quay, Roosevelt rounded up the Rough Riders and told them to board the transport as soon as it docked. Since two other regiments, a regular army infantry outfit and some New York volunteers, had previously been assigned to the *Yucatan*, a serious combat action was threatened even before the troops reached Cuba and the enemy. But Roosevelt, supported by his hard-fisted Rough Riders, persuaded the members of the other regiments that the Rough Riders were already in possession of the *Yucatan* and they meant to remain in possession.

Roosevelt then sent several details of men back to the coal cars to get the Rough Riders' baggage, food and ammunition. Thirty-six active hours after they left their camp at Tampa, the Rough Riders were aboard the *Yucatan* and anchored a half-mile offshore in Tampa harbor. There they settled back comfortably and demanded from every passing ship, "Where's the war?"

Their comfort was to be short-lived, however, for they were to remain anchored in Tampa harbor for almost a week in the sweltering heat, packed like sardines in a can and short of food and water, before all of the other transports were loaded and orders were given for the expedition to set sail.

There were a dozen or more navy warships and 32 transports in the convoy that carried about 16,000 men, most of whom had gone through the same ordeal as the Rough Riders during the past week. But curiously, as each of the 89 war correspondents in the convoy informed their readers, there was little or no grumbling. Every man aboard seemed delighted to be among the first to sail for Cuba, while thousands of their envious brothers in arms were forced to remain behind.

The convoy reached a point off Santiago early on June 20, 1898. Admiral Sampson wanted Shafter to land his Fifth Corps troops immediately, storm the harbor fortifications and drive the Spanish inland. Sampson then intended to enter Santiago Bay and attack Cervera and his Spanish warships. But insurgent General Garcia had strongly recommended that the Americans land their troops in force at a place called Daiquiri, about 18 miles from Santiago Bay. Because of Garcia's advice and because he did not want to attack a fortress without the support of U.S. artillery, Shafter decided to land at Daiquiri. This proved to be a wise, if a somewhat lucky, decision. The landing there was unopposed, a fatal mistake by the Spanish. Military historians agree that if the landing had been opposed, a disaster would have resulted for the U.S. troops.

If anything, the debarkation was more confused than the embarkation. Both operations took days when they should have taken hours. For the debarkation there were once again no plans. Regiments or parts of regiments were allowed to get ashore any way they could. Much equipment was abandoned or lost in the surf. Many civilian captains of the commercial ships that had been chartered as troopships not only refused to move their vessels inshore but also headed them out toward sea and had to be rounded up and driven back toward land by the U.S. Navy. Since there seemed to be no other way to get horses and mules ashore, they were simply dropped over the sides of the transports and allowed to sink or swim. Unfortunately, all too many tried to swim out to sea and drowned.

When Teddy Roosevelt saw what was happening to the animals, he urgently recommended that they be strung together with ropes before they were dropped overboard and then led ashore by men in motor launches. This system worked admirably.

By nightfall of June 22, less than half of General Shafter's forces were ashore, and the march on Santiago was scheduled to start the next day. Roosevelt urged Shafter to proceed on schedule, insisting that the Rough Riders would more than make up for the missing troops. Shafter agreed to move against the enemy the next day. The only problem now was that nobody knew exactly where the enemy was.

The Battle of San Juan Hill

According to the best information that General Shafter had, there were supposed to be more than 30,000 Spanish troops in the Santiago area, some 12,000 of them dug in around the city itself. Despite the fact that he did not know exactly where most of these troops were, Shafter decided to move directly toward Santiago by a road leading through the coastal village of Siboney.

Brigadier General Henry W. Lawton was placed in direct command of this operation, and he captured Siboney against light opposition on June 23. Lawton's forces then built up a strong semicircular defensive ring just inland from the Siboney beaches. This was done so that those men who had not landed in Daiquiri could now land at the protected beachhead at Siboney. This troop landing was successfully accomplished, and from that point on Siboney became the debarkation point for all of the expedition's men, animals and supplies.

While Lawton was consolidating his position at Siboney, Brigadier General Joseph "Fightin' Joe" Wheeler and his dismounted cavalry also marched toward Santiago. They were temporarily delayed by a small force of Spanish infantry at the village of Las Guasimas. Both sides suffered light casualties before the Spanish hastily retreated toward Santiago's strong outer defenses. As the Spanish troops retreated, General Wheeler, who had fought with the Confederate Army against the Yankee North in the Civil War, shouted the old Rebel cry, "Come on, men, we've got the damned Yanks on the run!" Former Yank soldiers now joined their Rebel brothers in responding enthusiastically to Fightin' Joe's war cry.

Shafter next began to make plans to overrun Santiago's outer defenses, which were built along high ridges topped by the San Juan Hill area. There was also a Spanish defense position in the village of El Caney to the north of San Juan.

Shafter's plan was for General Lawton's division to move out from Siboney and capture El Caney. This move, which would secure the American right flank, was intended to take no longer than a few hours. Shafter then planned to send his entire force against the San Juan Hill complex, which included nearby Kettle Hill. (Kettle Hill was not given its name by the Cubans or Spaniards. Actually, it was a knobby uprising that was part of the San Juan Hill complex

Major General William R. Shafter.

but separated from San Juan Hill proper. It was given its name by the Rough Riders who found a huge iron kettle on top of the hill which was probably used to refine sugar.) But the capture of El Caney was delayed because Shafter was unable to get his 300-pound bulk astride a horse. Plagued by the gout, which forced him to stomp about the battlefield with one foot in a grain sack, and later prostrated by the heat, Shafter was unable to take overall command of the engagement. Subordinate officers were called upon to direct and lead the attack. In addition, El Caney was gallantly defended by a brave band of 600 Spaniards led by the heroic General Joaquin del Ray.

Twice the blue-coated Spaniards in their straw sombreros stood shoulder to shoulder and fought off one of Lawton's entire regiments. Finally, however, the Americans wheeled up an artillery battery to shell the El Caney defenders, a handful of whom held out in a stone blockhouse. Sharpshooters were also assigned to pick off the fort's defenders one by one. In a short time, the El Caney fortress fell, but del Ray and a small detachment fought on outside the town until del Ray himself was killed. El Caney then surrendered.

Meanwhile, the attack on the San Juan heights area had been unable to proceed on schedule until the American right flank was secured. When El Caney fell and the San Juan attack did begin on the morning of July 1, 1898, it began in a confused fashion.

General Jacob Kent was in charge of an American infantry division that attacked San Juan Hill proper to

Brigadier General Henry W. Lawton, leader of attack at El Caney.

PHOTO: U.S. SIGNAL CORPS.

the left and General Samuel Sumner led a division of dismounted cavalry up Kettle Hill to the right. The dismounted cavalry units included not only Teddy Roosevelt and his Rough Riders but also a black cavalry regiment led by a young lieutenant named John J. Pershing, who would one day command the American Expeditionary Force in France in World War I. Because of his long service with the brave black troops, the young lieutenant was given the nickname, "Black Jack," a nickname of which young Pershing was extremely proud.

The confusion in the initial advance against the San Juan heights complex was caused by a U.S. Signal Corps captive observation balloon that was towed along by men in the advancing front line. The Spanish artillery zeroed in on the area over which the balloon hovered, and the accurate enemy shellfire disrupted the American advance. In addition, the American artillery was firing black powder ammunition (the Spanish used smokeless powder) and could be easily spotted and silenced by the Spanish heavy guns.

The extremely accurate enemy fire finally caused a U.S. volunteer regiment to panic. Many of the men also became exhausted from the intense heat. To reinforce the panicky volunteers and restore their morale, a regular army regiment of dismounted black cavalrymen was sent forward. These were Lieutenant Pershing's troopers, and they quickly stemmed the tide of retreating rookies and persuaded them to return to action.

*Infantry in San Juan Creek bottom under fire from San Juan Hill. A
private's pay was $13 a month.*

One volunteer regiment that did not panic, however, was Roosevelt's dismounted Rough Riders. Roosevelt himself was mounted on a noble little horse called Texas, who seemed as blissfully unaware of the shells falling around him as did his master. Moments before they went into action, Roosevelt rode up and down before his men, giving them a pep talk. As he spoke, he waved his men forward, brandishing a revolver that had been taken from the sunken battleship *Maine*. His words were greeted by a great cheer from his men.

Roosevelt held up his hand. "Don't cheer, boys," he said. "Fight! Now's the time to fight!"

Then the fearless Teddy wheeled his mount about and rode forward into battle. His men followed, trotting courageously behind him, and despite the hail of shot and shell, the Rough Riders moved unhesitatingly and stubbornly up the long slope. Soon even Roosevelt had to dismount because the tall jungle grass was too difficult for his horse to move through. Later, Roosevelt also had to discard his cavalry sword because it kept catching in the brush.

As Roosevelt and his men moved relentlessly forward, his men continued to shout cheers and cowboy yells, sounds that the Spaniards could hear above the roar of battle. These strange yells, and the Rough Riders' refusal to be halted by the withering hail of direct fire, caused the Spanish defenders to become fearful. No matter how many Americans went down, more seemed to come. They kept up their

Trenches of the Rough Riders on San Juan Hill.

PHOTO: U.S. SIGNAL CORPS.

relentless charge, firing as they ran until they seized the top of Kettle Hill, driving the enemy from their redoubts and down the opposite slopes beyond.

The battle won, the Rough Riders sprawled about on top of the hill, laughing and swearing. At this point Teddy Roosevelt moved among them and said, "Don't swear, boys. Get up there on the line and shoot." Roosevelt feared a counterattack by the enemy. But no such attack was forthcoming.

San Juan Hill proper, which was separated from and to the left of Kettle Hill, was not so readily taken. At the top of this hill were Spanish blockhouses, and from here the Spanish artillery had a free field of fire onto the open slope up which the American infantry had to advance. To advance in the open under the burning sun with only rifles and no supporting fire against the enemy artillery seemed suicidal. Finally, however, a young lieutenant named John H. Parker solved the problem.

Parker was in charge of a Gatling gun detachment. Gatling guns were automatic weapons on wheels that were somewhat like large machine guns. They had always been used for defensive fighting only, never in an advance. Parker thought they could be used in an advance and immediately set out to prove his point. Moving his guns into line, he joined the infantry attack, and the famous charge up San Juan Hill began.

Supported by the "coffee grinders," as the troops called the Gatling guns, the infantry regained its spirit

Parker's Gatling guns to the assault!

PHOTO: U.S. ARMY.

and moved forward at the double. Watching the relentless forward move by the Americans in the face of direct heavy fire, the Spanish general in command, Arsenio Linares, said, "They are very gallant and brave, these Americans, but very foolish." But it was just such foolish gallantry that won the day. By nightfall the San Juan Hill area was completely in American hands.

But it had been a costly victory. The United States forces, which numbered about 6,600 men, suffered more than 1,600 casualties, 225 killed and 1,400 wounded. Spanish casualties were less than half this number. The Rough Rider regiment of 490 men suffered 89 casualties.

With the fall of the village of El Caney and the San Juan Hill complex, U.S. troops now held all of the Santiago outer defenses. While the day's fighting had been going on, however, General Linares had been reinforcing his second line of defenses. And beyond these lay the city's inner defenses, which included great lengths of barbed wire.

The dispirited Shafter decided that these defenses were too difficult to take by frontal assault unless he received additional artillery to blast his way into the city. Shafter was also handicapped by the fact that he was by no means recovered from his heat prostration, and in addition, General Wheeler had fallen ill and was unable to lead his division. Unable to advance and forced to make their camps in relatively open areas, the Americans continued to take casualties as the

Infantry trenches on San Juan Hill.

PHOTO: U.S. SIGNAL CORPS.

Spanish gunners fired from their protected positions. Shafter also feared for the health and safety of his men, because of the malaria and yellow fever that were always threats in this area and because of the hurricane season which was about to begin. Shafter requested permission from the War Department to withdraw his troops to a more protected area several miles from the city. His request was refused. Now, not only unable to advance but also unable to retreat, Shafter did not know exactly what to do next.

He finally requested that the U.S. Navy ships outside Santiago harbor run the channel and attack the city from the bay. But Admiral Sampson refused to risk his ships in this fashion. He still feared bombardment from shore batteries and insisted that Shafter's forces continue to attack the city and silence these batteries. Since no one but President McKinley had authority over both the army and the navy and McKinley refused to interfere, a stalemate threatened to develop. At precisely this point the Spanish once again solved the Americans' problems, this time by making a bold but foolish attempt to sail their fleet out of Santiago harbor.

Cervera's Fatal Sortie

No one, least of all Spanish Admiral Cervera, expected the Spanish fleet bottled up in Santiago Bay to be suddenly forced into an immediate attempt to smash its way through the American naval blockade. But, with the fall of El Caney and San Juan, the Spanish authorities both in Cuba and in Spain began to fear the fall of Santiago. And if Santiago fell, Cervera's squadron would probably also have to surrender.

Cuba's governor general, Ramón Blanco, virtually ordered Cervera out of the harbor. When Cervera refused, Blanco consulted with authorities in Spain, who agreed that the Spanish squadron should attempt to escape and make its way to Havana. Such a move, they reasoned, would not only save the Spanish warships but would also draw the American land forces away from Santiago. On July 2, Cervera was again ordered to break the blockade. He had no choice but to obey orders.

Cervera had wanted to sail at night, but Admiral Sampson had illuminated the harbor with searchlights to prevent such a move. As a result, at 9:30 A.M. on the morning of July 3, Admiral Cervera aboard his flagship, *Maria Teresa*, emerged from Santiago harbor. Following the flagship at five-minute intervals—the sunken collier *Merrimac* forced the enemy ships to sail in single file through the narrow channel—were three cruisers, *Vizcaya*, *Cristóbal Colón* and *Oquendo*, and two destroyers, *Pluton* and *Furor*.

The Americans were taken by surprise by Cervera's sudden sortie, but they were not caught off guard. Admiral Sampson had worked out a very careful and efficient system for the blockade, so that each ship had its assigned place and responsibility at all times. If a ship was off its station while taking on coal about 50 miles away at Guantanamo, the ship that was next in line was charged with the duty of covering the open cruising space.

Sampson's foresighted plan paid off handsomely, because on the day of Cervera's sortie the battleship *Massachusetts* and the cruiser *Suwanee* were at Guantanamo. In addition, Sampson's flagship *New York* was also out of line while he was having a conference with General Shafter at Siboney, several miles to the east. When Sampson sailed for Siboney, he signaled the rest of the U.S. fleet: "Disregard movements of the commander-in-chief." Thus, when the first Spanish ship was sighted, Sampson's second in command, Commodore Schley, aboard the cruiser *Brooklyn*, instantly assumed command. He hoisted the signal, "Close up!" to the battleships *Iowa*, *Indiana*, *Oregon* and *Texas* and to two smaller armed vessels, *Vixen* and *Gloucester*. Although Schley's right to assume command seemed perfectly obvious, the question of his overall battle authority later resulted in a bitter dispute between him and Admiral Sampson.

A lookout aboard the battleship *Iowa* was the first to sight the *Maria Teresa*. *Iowa's* gunners immediately opened fire, while "general quarters" was sounded throughout the rest of the fleet. Within moments virtually all of the ships in both fleets were firing at each other, and even the Spanish harbor batteries joined in the bombardment. But American gunnery was obviously far superior to the enemy's. Badly damaged, Cervera's *Maria Teresa* tried to ram Schley's *Brooklyn*, hoping to make a gap in the battle line through which the rest of the Spanish fleet might escape to Havana or even find a closer haven at Cienfuegos. The *Vizcaya* also tried to ram the *Brooklyn*, but Schley neatly maneuvered away from his attackers while the rest of the American warships concentrated their fire on the *Maria Teresa*. Moments later Cervera's daring dash for freedom ended in disaster.

By 10:15 the shattered *Maria Teresa*, on fire and listing badly, was ordered beached by Cervera. By 10:20 the *Oquendo*, after a brief but decisive duel with the *Texas*, also accepted defeat and turned toward the beach. The *Brooklyn* and the *Oregon* now took out after the *Vizcaya* and *Cristóbal Colón*, while the slower Ameri-

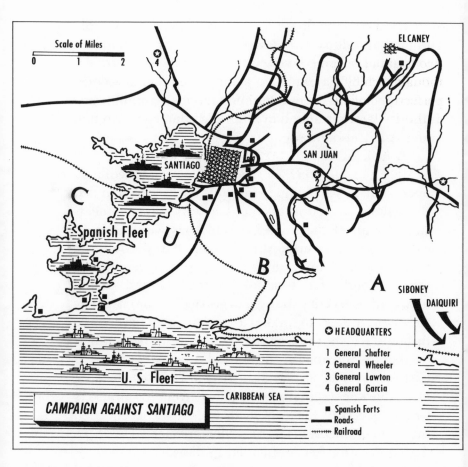

CAMPAIGN AGAINST SANTIAGO

can warships pursued and sank the Spanish destroyers, *Furor* and *Pluton*. At 11:15 the *Vizcaya*, riddled by shellfire, was driven ashore and its crew captured.

By this time Admiral Sampson, aboard the *New York*, was able to join the fray, but it was the fast-moving *Oregon* that was able to overtake the swift *Colón* and drive it ashore about 45 miles down the coast. This action lasted until 1:30 P.M., but when it was over the American victory was complete. Aboard the American ships cheers went up as bands played the national anthem. But the captain of the *Texas*, John Philip, told his men, "Don't cheer, men—the poor chaps are dying." Immediately the victorious U.S. sailors began to rescue their recent enemies from the sea.

There were about 2,200 Spanish sailors in this engagement and about the same number of Americans. Some 323 Spaniards were killed, 151 were wounded and most of the remainder—about 1,750—were taken prisoner either in the rescue operation or through outright surrender. U.S. casualties were one man killed and one slightly wounded. No U.S. ship was badly damaged. The lone U.S. fatality was Chief Yeoman G. H. Ellis of Schley's flagship *Brooklyn*.

Completely ignoring Schley's role as a key figure in the outstanding naval victory, Sampson wired Washington:

THE FLEET UNDER MY COMMAND OFFERS THE NATION, AS A FOURTH OF JULY PRESENT, THE WHOLE OF CERVERA'S FLEET.

Admiral William T. Sampson.

PHOTO: U.S. BUREAU OF SHIPS.

Sampson's message caused great celebration throughout the United States. It also caused a considerable amount of controversy when it became known that it had actually been Schley who had been in immediate command of the victorious U.S. war fleet. The controversy continued for many months after the war, despite the fact that the generous and open-hearted Schley insisted that Sampson had been the architect of the battle plan and that he, Schley, and the other ship captains had merely executed it. There was, in the end, more than enough credit for all to share, and decorations and promotions were made throughout the fleet.

Following the destruction of the Spanish squadron, it now was up to General Shafter to capture the city of Santiago itself.

The Surrender of Santiago

The Spanish troops, as well as Cuban civilians, inside the besieged city of Santiago now found themselves in an all but hopeless situation. Both food and ammunition were low, and with the destruction of Cervera's fleet there was no further hope of resupplying the city. In addition, the Spanish garrison commander, General Linares, had been wounded and was unable to remain in active charge of Santiago's defenses. Linares was replaced by General José Toral, and it was with Toral whom Shafter dealt in trying to obtain a Spanish surrender.

The U.S. War Department wanted Shafter to bombard the city into submission, but Shafter resisted for humanitarian reasons. He did not want to subject helpless civilians to a bombardment. He was also aware of the fact that Lieutenant Hobson and his crew from the sunken *Merrimac* were being held prisoner somewhere in Santiago, and their lives would be endangered by a general bombardment.

General Shafter did, however, arrange with General Toral for a truce, and the two generals met between the lines—Shafter was now able to ride a horse—where Shafter did his best to convince Toral that unconditional surrender was his only choice. Toral then returned to consult with the wounded Linares, who in turn consulted with Spanish officials in Madrid, requesting permission to surrender. Technically, Spanish commanders were not allowed to surrender as long as they were able to mount any kind of an attack, but Linares tried to persuade his superiors that further resistance was out of the question.

Meanwhile, on July 10, Shafter permitted his army field artillery to join a naval bombardment of the city. In addition, U.S. Army Commanding General Nelson Miles arrived in Cuba with troop reinforcements. The purpose of Miles's move was to make certain that he could take part in Cuban combat before it was all over, so that he, too, could share in the glory of victory over the Spanish. The combined army-navy bombardment, plus Miles's arrival with reinforcements, almost convinced Toral's superiors that he must be allowed to surrender.

What finally did convince them was an extremely generous offer made by U.S. Secretary of War Alger. In return for unconditional surrender, Alger offered the Spanish troops transportation back to Spain in troop transports that the U.S. government would pay for. Most of the Spanish soldiers had not seen their homes in Spain in several years, and many doubted that they would ever see them again. Alger's offer was too good to refuse.

General Shafter also wanted to let the Spanish keep their weapons, but the War Department would not allow this. Finally, not only the Santiago troops were included in the surrender terms but also all of the Spanish troops throughout the area. This included some 25,000 men along with their cannon, rifles, ammunition and a small store of military equipment and supplies.

The surrender ceremony—a brief one—took place on July 17, 1898, when Shafter and a troop of cavalry met Toral and an accompanying garrison guard of about 100 men just outside of Santiago. Toral and his guard turned over their personal weapons to the Americans, and the Spanish surrendered the city they had held for almost four centuries. A few weeks later, while the two countries were actually still at war, the troopships paid for by the United States began to carry the defeated Spanish troops back to Spain—a unique operation in military history.

Historians have since agreed that if the Spanish had been able to hold out just a short time longer at Santiago, the tide of battle might well have turned, because it was only after the surrender that the Americans faced their worst enemy. This was disease in the form of malaria, typhoid fever and yellow fever.

When the Spanish had left Santiago, General

Surrender of Santiago.

PHOTO: U.S. SIGNAL CORPS.

Shafter and all of his commanders assumed that they, too, would soon be leaving for home. But the War Department officials saw it otherwise. They wanted Shafter's army to act as a kind of army of occupation in and around Santiago—at least until General Miles had completed the Cuban campaign by taking over Porto Rico. (The spelling did not become Puerto Rico until after 1932.) Shafter tried to make clear that there was absolutely no point to the War Department's decision since all resistance had ended at Santiago and General Miles and 3,000 troops were already embarked on the Porto Rican expedition.

Teddy Roosevelt added his voice to Shafter's by observing that if the army was kept in Cuba, three-quarters of the men would die or become permanent invalids. That Roosevelt wasn't exaggerating was indicated by the fact that in late July, Shafter reported 4,255 men sick, 3,164 of whom had the deadly yellow fever. The remainder had malaria or typhoid fever, and virtually all of the troops were suffering from dysentery, caused by poor sanitation and food poisoning.

When the War Department continued to turn a deaf ear to the sick and dying Americans in Cuba, several of Shafter's officers proceeded to take matters into their own hands. Man of action that he was, Roosevelt was among the ringleaders in this action. A joint, or so-called round-robin, letter was written by Roosevelt and signed by a group of Roosevelt's fellow officers demanding the immediate evacuation of the

Yellow fever hospital (in tents).

PHOTO: U.S. SIGNAL CORPS.

army from Cuba. In part, the round robin read: "This army must be moved at once or it will perish. As an army it can be safely moved now. Persons responsible for preventing such a move will be responsible for the unnecessary loss of many thousands of lives."

The somewhat mutinous letter was actually addressed and sent personally to General Shafter, who was supposed to forward it to top army officials in Washington. But Roosevelt was instrumental in seeing to it that a copy fell into the hands of an Associated Press reporter. As a result, the letter was printed in newspapers throughout the United States even before the original reached Washington. It caused an immediate sensation, and War Department officials began to fall all over themselves in their haste to "get the boys out of Cuba."

The American troops based at Santiago, including the Rough Riders, were almost immediately brought home and placed in a huge quarantined camp on Montauk Point at the tip of Long Island. More than 20,000 of the 35,000 men who were processed at Montauk Point were ill. Fortunately, most of them recovered. However, of the approximately 5,000 men in the United States forces who lost their lives during the course of the entire war, some 4,600 died of disease. The only good thing to grow out of this tragic experience was that it led to a study of tropical diseases by Dr. Walter Reed and William Crawford Gorgas that resulted in the virtual elimination of the yellow fever scourge. Without Reed and Gorgas's findings the

Infantry encampment before San Juan Hill. Food was mainly stringy, tasteless canned boiled beef (not corned beef) meant to be eaten as a stew with vegetables. There were seldom any vegetables, so the men ate the "embalmed beef" straight from the can.

PHOTO: U.S. SIGNAL CORPS.

Panama Canal could probably never have been built.

Ironically, it was only after they were returned from the hot, wet tropics and recovering at Montauk Point, where it was relatively cool and dry, that the Rough Riders could remove their heavy woolen uniforms and replace them with the newly issued cotton uniforms. As they had about most discomforts in the past, the Rough Riders made light of this situation. The one thing about which they worried, as they convalesced during the next several months and began to think of returning to civilian life, was what to do with their remaining mascots.

During the course of the brief but bitter part of the war in which they had been engaged, the Rough Riders had had a whole series of mascots—both human and animal. Some of these were still with them. Others had been left behind.

They had begun to collect these mascots while still at Tampa, before embarking for Cuba. Among them were several small boys, including a twelve-year-old lad named Dabney Royster, who was from Tennessee. Not only did the soldiers adopt him, but they also fitted him out in a special Rough Rider's uniform. When the regiment had sailed for Cuba, young Royster had secretly stowed away aboard the troopship along with his own junior-sized rifle and several boxes of cartridges. Fortunately, the boy was discovered before the convoy sailed, but he was heartbroken when the equally saddened Rough Riders put him back ashore. They were never to see him again.

Among the mascots who were still with the Rough Riders when they reached Montauk Point were a mountain lion, an eagle and a mongrel dog. The mountain lion was named Josephine and had been brought with them by Arizona cowboys when they first joined the regiment. The eagle had been brought by the troopers from New Mexico and was called Teddy Roosevelt. The mongrel was called Cuba and had followed faithfully at Teddy Roosevelt's heels all during the campaign.

All of these animals had given the Rough Riders endless delight, and they continued to do so during their masters' convalescence at the Long Island camp. Josephine, the mountain lion, had never stopped trying to capture Teddy, the eagle, and eat him for lunch, but Teddy was every bit as fierce and resourceful as the Teddy Roosevelt for whom he had been named, and constantly escaped the lion's jaws. Although the Rough Riders tried to keep Josephine tied up, the dog Cuba constantly teased Josephine until she would manage to break loose. On one such occasion, Josephine escaped and made her way into the company area of a neighboring regiment. There she climbed into bed with an off-duty trooper who was napping in his tent. When the unsuspecting trooper was awakened by Josephine licking his face, the victim's yells could be heard throughout the camp. But Josephine was as startled as the trooper and bounded away and dashed back to her Rough Rider friends with no real harm done to either man or animal. It

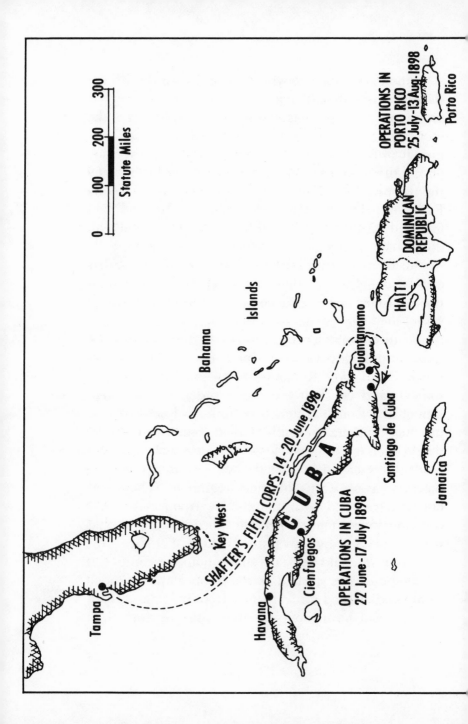

was after this incident, however, that Roosevelt decided that the mascots—with the exception of the dog Cuba whom he kept for his own pet—had to be given to a New York zoo.

Meanwhile, the picnic that everybody had expected to attend in Cuba was occurring in Porto Rico.

General Miles invaded Porto Rico on July 26, 1898. Actually, it was not so much an invasion as an occupation since it was almost a bloodless campaign. One sharp engagement was fought at Guanica on the southeast coast of the island, but there were few serious casualties. On July 28, Miles and his men moved on to nearby Ponce, which offered no opposition, and this was turned into the main army base.

Reinforcements under General John R. Brooke were landed at Guayama, and soon the entire island was overrun. Rather than opposition, the American troops met with such wild enthusiasm that the only serious problem that arose was finding enough American flags and red, white and blue bunting to give to the people so they could decorate their homes and public buildings. When word of the Porto Rican picnic reached the United States, volunteer troops that had not yet seen action again began to clamor to get into combat before a peace treaty could be signed that would end all of the fun.

There yet remained one major action of the war to be fought. This was the battle for Manila in the Philippines.

The Fall of
the Philippines

When reports of Admiral Dewey's destruction of the Spanish war fleet in Manila harbor had reached the United States at the start of the war, most Americans thought that Dewey had captured the whole of the Philippine Islands. This was far from true. In fact, all Dewey had done was all that he was capable of doing without any land forces at his command: He had set up and maintained a rigid blockade of Manila.

After his great naval victory over the Spanish, Dewey had sent a message to Washington on May 13, 1898, requesting 5,000 troops "to take possession of and control the Philippine Islands." Dewey also reported that a number of other nations had ships in the area observing American naval activity. These included war vessels from Great Britain, France, Germany and Japan. These men-of-war observer ships were to cause Dewey and the United States a consider-

Admiral George Dewey, hero of Manila, in dress uniform.

PHOTO: U.S. BUREAU OF SHIPS.

able amount of concern during the next several months.

Another cause of concern was Emilio Aguinaldo, leader of the Philippine insurgents or rebels who had carried on a long campaign for independence against the local Spanish rulers. Like the Cuban rebels, the insurgent Filipinos assumed that the United States would aid them in their fight for freedom. While this was true to a certain degree, a number of American leaders—among them President McKinley—saw Dewey's victory as a golden opportunity to take over or annex the Philippines. Control of the Philippines would, in one great stroke, make the United States not only a major power in the Pacific but also a major world power.

One step in this imperialistic direction was already about to take place with the annexation of Hawaii by the United States, which was scheduled for early July. Most Hawaiians, however, were in favor of annexation, while Aguinaldo and his fellow Filipino insurgents were not. On July 1, Aguinaldo took matters into his own hands and declared himself president of the new Philippine Republic. If the Philippines were to become the spoils of a victorious war against Spain to free Cuba, Washington officials realized that Aguinaldo must somehow be brought under control by American land forces.

Although Dewey had made his request for 5,000 troops in mid-May, it wasn't until early July that the first 2,500 of these men arrived at Manila. (The bloodless capture of the island of Guam was accomplished along the way—a further indication of the United States' growing power in the Pacific. Guam would be the site of fierce fighting in World War II.) These men were commanded by General Thomas M. Anderson. They were soon reinforced by a second contingent of 3,500 men under General Francis V. Greene, and finally a third contingent of some 5,000 men under General Arthur MacArthur. Arthur MacArthur was the father of General Douglas MacArthur, who was to become the famed hero of the Pacific fighting against the Japanese during World War II. The overall commander of this expedition against the Spanish in the Philippines was General Wesley Merritt.

When General Merritt sailed from San Francisco, he and his amphibious force faced several problems. The first was to prevail upon the Spanish in Manila to surrender without a prolonged siege. The second was to avoid offending rebel leader Aguinaldo when it became clear to him that the United States did not intend to immediately recognize his self-proclaimed Philippine Republic.

Aguinaldo had already threatened to attack Manila on his own, and a bloodbath was almost certain to follow such action. Dewey had informed Merritt, however, that he was certain that Aguinaldo had neither the arms nor ammunition to carry out such an attack. Merritt's third problem was what to do if his troopships and their escorts encountered a last Spanish war fleet that was reported to have sailed from Cadiz, Spain, bound for the Philippines to intercept Merritt's convoy.

The movement of the last of the Spanish warships from Cadiz had been prompted by the activities of several of the foreign observer ships at Manila that had been watching Dewey's fleet and reporting its activities back to their own countries. Most active among these observer vessels were five men-of-war belonging to Germany, who also hoped to share in some of the Philippine spoils that were bound to result from the war. The five German ships under Admiral Otto von Diederichs kept in close communication with the Spanish in Manila, who relayed von Diederichs's information back to Madrid. The German vessels also sailed close enough inshore to fire shells into the ranks of the rebels, who by now had all but surrounded Manila from the rear. The Germans thus indicated that they were allied with Spain against the Americans.

It was the apparent support being offered by the German warships at Manila harbor that had prompted Spanish officials to order the last of Spain's fleet to the Philippines. This fleet was under the command of Admiral Manuel de la Camara and consisted of 12 warships, several more than Dewey had at his command. If they reached Manila and defeated Dewey—perhaps with aid from the German fleet already at Manila—the troop convoy sailing from the United States would be at the mercy of the Spanish when it reached the Philippines.

Such an eventuality never came to pass for two reasons. First, Admiral Sir Edward Chichester and his two Royal Navy observer ships at Manila kept a weather eye on the Germans. When it seemed that a crisis had been reached, Chichester—without actually committing His Majesty's government to such an action—implied to the German fleet commander that if hostilities broke out between the German force and Dewey's force, the British ships would come to the immediate support of Dewey. Dewey also told Admiral von Diederichs, "If you want war, I'm ready." The German admiral quickly backed away from the threatened conflict since he, too, had no authorization from his government for such action, and Germany definitely did not want war.

Second, when word of the Spanish fleet's sailing for the Philippines reached the United States, an American naval squadron under Admiral J. C. Watson was immediately dispatched for Spain, where it threatened to attack the Spanish coast. Now it was the people in Spanish coastal cities who reacted, just as violently as had the Americans along the eastern seaboard at the threat of raids by Cervera's Spanish squadron at the start of the war.

Camara's fleet had sailed as far as the Red Sea by late June. As Watson's fleet reached the mid-Atlantic, the Spanish reaction at home was so violent that Spanish officials were forced to recall Camara the first week in July.

The main threat that now lay ahead of Merritt's amphibious forces occupying Manila and taking over control of the Philippines was a bloodbath that might result from U.S. troops fighting against Spanish troops if the Spanish commander refused to surrender. A serious secondary threat was the possibility of Aguinaldo's rebel forces being provoked into a premature attack against the Spanish. If this occurred, Merritt and Dewey would be hard pressed to decide whether they, too, should attack the Spanish or Aguinaldo and his Filipino insurgents—or both.

Aguinaldo was angry at the American troop buildup that had reached more than 11,000 men by the end of July. He knew that as the American forces grew in strength, his own bargaining position as a threat against the Spanish grew weaker. Both Merritt and Dewey knew this, too, and they decided to take Manila with as little aid as possible from the Filipino insurgents.

Merritt's problems were further complicated by the fact that, in order to get at Manila by land, American troops would have to move through lines of Filipino insurgents surrounding the city. To accomplish this feat took great skill and tact on Merritt's part. In the end he called upon Admiral Dewey to conclude the diplomatic negotiations with Aguinaldo. Dewey had dealt with Aguinaldo before and had decided that when all else failed a direct order usually got the proper response from the rebel leader. In this case Dewey finally ordered Aguinaldo to move his troops out and let the Americans move in. Aguinaldo accepted the order, but grudgingly. His troops responded

General Wesley Merritt.

PHOTO: U.S. SIGNAL CORPS.

with equal reluctance and moved out slowly. The Americans would hear from Aguinaldo and his forces again.

Negotiations with the Spanish were rapidly brought to a conclusion by the end of July. As had been the case at Santiago, the Spanish commanders felt honor-bound not to surrender except in the case of an enemy assault. In this instance the "assault" was provided, on August 9, by a brief bombardment from Dewey's naval guns. Their honor appeased, the Spanish prepared to surrender, and on August 12 the American troops advanced peacefully toward Manila.

At this point, however, firing broke out from the American lines against the Spanish. It was not definitely known who started the firing, but it was generally thought to be the Filipino insurgents, some of whom were still intermingled among the American troops. In any event, for a brief period Merritt feared general fighting might break out. But, when there was no return fire from the Spanish, the peaceful American advance was continued. On August 12 Manila capitulated, but formal surrender terms were not signed until August 14. None of the participants in the surrender ceremony realized that the war had actually ended two days earlier when Spain had sued the United States for peace.

To all intents and purposes the Spanish-American War had now ended, although the official peace treaty would not be signed until December 10, 1898, in Paris. (The treaty was not ratified by the United States

Senate until February 6, 1899, and then only by a one-vote margin. The delay and the close final vote were caused by the fact that there was much strong anti-imperialistic feeling in the United States against the annexation of the Philippines.) By the treaty's terms, Porto Rico and Guam were ceded outright to the United States. Cuba was given its freedom, but the United States was permitted to occupy the island until a sovereign government could be established there. In return for a payment of $20 million, the Philippine Islands were also ceded to the United States.

While the United States and Spain officially recognized the formalized terms of this treaty, Aguinaldo and his Filipino followers most certainly did not. They were more determined than ever to continue their fight for freedom against all oppressors, Spanish or American. Early in 1899, just when the United States Senate was preparing to ratify the Treaty of Paris, Aguinaldo and his insurgents struck against Manila.

The Philippine Insurrection

After the U.S. Army took over Manila from the defeated Spanish, Aguinaldo set up his own Filipino capital about 30 miles away, at Malolos. He had at his command between 30,000 and 40,000 troops—some estimates went as high as 80,000—while effective American forces numbered only about 12,000 or 14,000. The insurgents, however, lacked arms and ammunition. Many of the Filipinos had no weapons except spears and bolo knives—long, heavy, saberlike blades somewhat like a machete but with only a single knife edge.

During the peace negotiations between the United States and Spain, General Merritt was called to Paris and General Elwell S. Otis succeeded him in the Philippines. When Otis took command, there were actually more than 21,000 U.S. Army troops in Manila, but almost half of these were volunteers scheduled to be sent home with the official end of the Spanish-American War at hand.

Now Otis was faced with a rebellion or insurrection that was even more dangerous and whose outcome was even less certain than the war just concluded. Otis immediately requested 40,000 additional "effectives for the field," but this request was slow in being filled. Eventually he did receive a dozen regiments of volunteers, two of them composed of black troops.

Manila was still the only Philippine area completely controlled by the United States. Aguinaldo on the other hand now had many of his troops stationed in blockhouses in a semicircular ring around Manila just as they had surrounded the Spanish. In addition, his loyal followers, both civilian and military, had spread Aguinaldo's control throughout most of the islands. But a major weapon on the American side was the active presence of the U.S. Navy against which Aguinaldo's insurrectionists, or so-called *insurrectos*, had no defense. Because of the U.S. Navy, most of the fighting during the insurrection was confined to the island of Luzon.

No one knew who fired the first shot, but on the late afternoon of February 4, 1899, general hostilities began between the Americans and the Filipino *insurrectos*. Somewhat to the surprise of the Filipinos who attacked Manila, the American response was quick and powerful. Not only did the U.S. Army fight back immediately and with fierce determination during the first afternoon and evening, but it also counterattacked at dawn the next day. The Filipinos were not used to this kind of fighting. Traditionally, they had fought against the Spanish late in the day and at night, and then both sides had rested through the tropical heat of the following day.

For the daylight attack, General Otis divided his 14,000 men into two divisions, one commanded by General Arthur MacArthur and the other commanded by General Thomas Anderson. They were supported by artillery, Gatling guns and ships' batteries from the U.S. Navy. The battle lasted two days, but it was actually no contest. When it was over, the *insurrectos* were totally shattered and running for the hills. They had suffered at least 3,000 casualties, the United States about 250. General Otis was prepared to declare that the brief "native revolt" had been smashed and the fighting ended. He and his men soon discovered, however, that the fighting had just begun.

As they had done so often in fighting against the Spanish in the past, the *insurrectos* now resorted to guerrilla warfare. Their roadless, tropical land was ideally suited to this type of fighting, and there was no way a major American offensive could be mounted against small bands of Filipinos who struck secretly by night or set up ambushes by daylight along jungle trails, struck silently and disappeared into the tropical forests. Artillery and naval gun barrages were futile against such furtive attacks, and Gatling guns soon had to be abandoned since they could not be hauled through the thick and all but impenetrable tropical undergrowth.

Nevertheless, the orthodox Otis continued to try and fight a rule-book and training-manual war. During the next seven months some additional 35,000 American troops arrived in the Philippines, and Otis used them in carefully planned set-piece attacks—the kind of attacks he had learned on the plains of West Point. The Filipinos stealthily cut the Americans to ribbons by nibbling at their flanks, cutting down a handful of men here, another handful there, with silent and vicious swings of their bolo knives, or by dropping them a man at a time with spears hurled with deadly accuracy from great distances. American morale began seriously to deteriorate as casualties mounted at the hands of an unseen foe—a murderous experience Americans would again have one day in fighting the Vietcong during the Vietnam war.

But there were still a number of American soldiers in the U.S. Army who had fought in the West and Southwest during the Indian Wars, and the training and experience these men had gone through against the redmen now payed off. The scouts and Indian fighters had learned that the art of survival in guerrilla warfare depended upon speed, daring, cunning, surprise and, above all, self-reliance and individual initiative to the point of recklessness. In the Philippines this type of frontier fighting again came to the fore.

Among those men who sprang from this old Indian-fighting tradition were a red-haired colonel, Frederick Funston, and his Twentieth Regiment of Kansas volunteers. In the spring of 1899, General MacArthur's division succeeded in capturing Aguinaldo's capital at Malolos. MacArthur then proceeded to move north in an attempt to capture both the fleeing Aguinaldo and his Filipino aide, General José Luna.

Aguinaldo and Luna and their forces retreated until they reached two parallel rivers, the Bagbag and the Rio Grande. On the far banks of these two rivers they prepared defenses in depth. Luna's men destroyed the center span of a railroad bridge across the Bagbag and then used the railroad ties and steel tracks from the bridge to erect fortresslike entrenchments on the river's opposite side. Aguinaldo's men moved on to the Rio Grande, where they also destroyed part of a bridge and used the remains to construct similar defensive entrenchments.

Colonel Funston and his Twentieth Regiment Kansans formed the "point" that spearheaded MacArthur's division in pursuit of Aguinaldo and Luna and their Filipino *insurrectos*. The Americans were supported by a naval gun that had been put aboard an armored train, but when the Bagbag River and its partially destroyed bridge were reached, there was no way for this gun nor the accompanying troops to cross the deep, 200-foot-wide river. The American advance was apparently stopped.

Calling for volunteers, Colonel Funston decided to seize the damaged bridge. Ten men joined him. Leaving the safety of the sheltering bamboo thickets that lined the river bank, Funston and his squad dashed for the near end of the bridge while the naval gun aboard its railroad car and the rest of the regiment covered them with heavy supporting fire.

A patrol in search of Aguinaldo.

PHOTO: U.S. SIGNAL CORPS.

Once on the bridge, the courageous Kansans crawled along the girders until they reached the broken span. Still covered by heavy fire, Funston and his men left their own weapons on the bridge, dived into the river and swam toward the enemy. But the enemy was already beginning to leave their barricades under the pounding of the naval gun and the extremely rapid rifle fire. When they reached the far bank, Funston and his weaponless Kansans charged the entrenchments. Fortunately, they found them empty of the enemy but filled with rifles and ammunition that the fleeing Filipinos had left behind. Funston waved the rest of the Americans across the Bagbag. Then he and his men moved forward toward the Rio Grande.

If anything, the Rio Grande presented an even more formidable obstacle than the Bagbag. It was equally deep and at least 200 feet wider. Here, however, Funston found a raft. Two of his men stripped and swam across the river carrying a rope. They fastened this rope to some pilings on the other side, and Funston used the rope to pull the raft across the Rio Grande by a hand-over-hand effort. The raft could only hold half a dozen men, but this time they could carry their rifles with them. The crossings were made under heavy fire by both sides, the *insurrectos* trying to stop the Americans and the Americans trying to protect the men aboard the crude troop ferry.

In spite of the odds, Funston's Kansans soon controlled the enemy river bank, and within two more days MacArthur's entire division had crossed the river on newly built rafts or by swimming. But, by the time the division was again ready to move out in force, Aguinaldo, Luna and most of the *insurrectos* had faded away into the sheltering jungle.

Funston had become completely convinced that the only way the insurrection could be put down was to capture or kill Aguinaldo. Funston was equally convinced that the only way to accomplish this was with a small force of men and probably through the use of a ruse or trick. But soon the monsoon or rainy season had set in—more than 70 inches of rain fell during the next several months—and neither side was able to resume full-scale fighting until the autumn of 1899.

The Capture of Aguinaldo

Although the rainy season caused a temporary halt in the major fighting, Filipino guerrilla attacks increased in number and ferocity. In addition, the *insurrectos* began to make Indian-style, hit-and-run raids on U.S. Army camps, taking prisoners and carrying them off to nearby villages to be tortured to death. When the Americans retaliated by raiding these villages, it was all but impossible for them to distinguish *insurrecto* soldiers from civilians. All too often the mutilated bodies of American prisoners were found, and the U.S. soldiers' reaction was to kill everybody in sight—men, women and children—and then burn the villages to the ground. Soon both sides were engaged in committing brutal atrocities with no quarter asked or given. This, too, was a forerunner of the barbarous actions by both sides during the future war in Vietnam.

In the Philippine fighting, perhaps the most brutal

torture of all was devised by the Americans. This was called the water treatment or water cure. When an *insurrecto* prisoner was taken, he was asked to give out certain military information—his organization, its size, the physical condition of its soldiers, the name of its commander and so on. (It was in this way that Funston hoped to learn the whereabouts of Aguinaldo.) If the prisoner refused to give this information, he was seized by his guards and several gallons of water were forced down his throat. Then he was spread-eagled on his back, and his inquisitors either kneeled or stood on his stomach, forcing out the water. This process was repeated until the prisoner either talked or died. Results were approximately fifty-fifty. Ironically, the United States had gone to war with Spain to put a stop to similar treatment of the Cubans by men under the command of "Butcher" Weyler.

It was not through the torture of Filipino prisoners, however, that the secret of Aguinaldo's whereabouts was discovered. This information was given by a Filipino traitor and then only after many more months of fighting.

When the dry season set in again in October 1899, General Otis resumed his full-scale assault against the *insurrectos*. Its purpose was to drive the enemy out of the entire island of Luzon. Initially the drive was highly successful, so successful that Otis was prepared to announce, "The so-called Filipino Republic is destroyed." But once again the announcement of the death of Aguinaldo's army and government was somewhat premature. The fighting went on, and both sides continued to suffer severe casualties both from combat and disease.

During the next year, more than 1,000 separate engagements were fought, and yet the end of the insurrection seemed no closer than it had when fighting first broke out. Aguinaldo remained as elusive as ever, and the flame of freedom burned even more brightly in the breasts of his Filipino followers.

At this point President McKinley stepped in and attempted to solve the problem. Since the military had been unable to bring order out of the chaos of the Philippines, McKinley decided to appoint a civil governor to accomplish the feat. The man he selected was a judge, William Howard Taft. Taft, a future president of the United States, rivaled General Shafter in weight—both tipped the scales at about 300 pounds— but Taft outweighed Shafter in administrative ability.

Upon Taft's arrival in the Philippines in the spring of 1900, General Otis resigned and was replaced by General MacArthur. While MacArthur made military plans to subdue the insurrectionists, Taft proceeded to put into effect civil plans to subdue them. Schools were constructed, villages were restored, medical aid was increased and a simple system of self-government modeled on democratic principles was established for those who took an oath of allegiance to the United States. Taft's efforts were extremely successful, but they could never be wholly successful as long as Aguinaldo and his *insurrecto* soldiers remained at large.

Early in 1901, Funston—a general officer now—and his Kansans captured one of Aguinaldo's messengers, Cecilio Segismundo. Although they were later accused of doing so, Funston and his officers stoutly denied that they had used the water treatment or any other form of torture on Segismundo. They insisted that Segismundo represented a faction of the *insurrectos* who were weary of the war and wanted it to end, even if it meant turning traitor to Aguinaldo and his cause. Segismundo said that Aguinaldo's headquarters were located at a village named Palinan in northeastern Luzon. Segismundo also said that he had been on his way to pick up a detachment of *insurrecto* guerrilla reinforcements whom he was to escort to Aguinaldo's headquarters.

When General Funston heard this, he knew that at last he had a ruse that would result in the capture of the *insurrecto* leader.

Funston had one of his aides write a letter to Aguinaldo using the forged signature of an insurgent leader, Ramón Lacuna. In the letter "Lacuna" said that he and Segismundo and their troops had captured five top American officers. These officers, the forged letter added, were being brought to Aguinaldo's headquarters by Segismundo and the reinforcements Aguinaldo had been expecting. Funston, of course, planned to include himself among the five "captives."

Funston's next problem was to assemble an "insurgent" guard from among the Filipino troops who were loyal to the Americans. Those he selected were from a

General Frederick Funston, Aguinaldo's captor. Funston's premature death just before start of World War I prevented his being named commander of the American Expeditionary Force to France. General John J. Pershing, another veteran of the Spanish-American War, was chosen Commander of the World War I AEF instead. Regarding black troops which he commanded as a lieutenant in Cuba, Pershing said, "White regiments and black regiments fought shoulder to shoulder, unmindful of race or color and mindful only of their common duty as Americans."

PHOTO: U.S. SIGNAL CORPS.

tribe called the Maccabebes, who were hereditary enemies of the Tagalog tribe, who were loyal to Aguinaldo. Funston had these Maccabebe troops dressed in captured *insurrecto* uniforms, and the party set out for Aguinaldo's headquarters early in February 1901.

It took Funston's party and their disguised Maccabebes almost two months to complete the journey through some of the most rugged jungle country in the Philippines. Along the way they were hailed as heroes by Aguinaldo loyalists through whose villages they had to pass. When at long last they reached Palinan, Aguinaldo sent out an *insurrecto* honor guard to greet them. Aguinaldo remained hidden in a house at the center of the village.

As the honor guard approached the Maccabebes and their American "prisoners," the Maccabebes stepped aside and let the members of the *insurrecto* honor guard make their way forward until they were surrounded. Then, guided by a signal from Segismundo, Funston and his fellow American officers dashed for the house in which Aguinaldo was hiding. As soon as the Americans were out of their line of fire, the Maccabebes raised their rifles and fired at point-blank range into the ranks of the surprised *insurrecto* honor guard. Hearing the firing and thinking his men had decided to stage some sort of celebration over the arrival of the American prisoners at Palinan, Aguinaldo shouted out of a window, "Stop wasting your ammunition!"

Until that moment Funston and his men were not exactly certain where Aguinaldo was. Now they dashed inside the house, overpowered the insurgent leader's bodyguard and wrestled Aguinaldo to the floor. Funston was hard pressed to keep his fellow officers from killing Aguinaldo because they thought he was responsible for all of the Filipino atrocities. Funston finally succeeded in saving Aguinaldo by throwing his body on top of him and ordering his men to hold their fire.

Aguinaldo was captured on March 23, 1901. Less than a week later he was taken to Manila and paraded in triumph through the streets. On April 19 he not only gave his oath of allegiance to the United States, but he also stated:

After mature deliberation, I resolutely proclaim to the world that I cannot refuse to heed the voice of a people longing for peace, nor the lamentations of thousands of families yearning to see their dear ones enjoying the liberty and promised generosity of the great American nation. By acknowledging and accepting the sovereignty of the United States throughout the Philippine Archipelago, as I now do, and without reservation whatsoever, I believe that I am serving thee, my beloved country.

But Aguinaldo's capture did not end the Philippine Insurrection. Although Aguinaldo called upon his *insurrecto* comrades to lay down their arms, they refused to do so. With blind and hopeless dedication they continued their guerrilla activities.

114

Emilio Aguinaldo some months after his capture.

PHOTO: U.S. SIGNAL CORPS.

Meanwhile, additional American troops from the Philippines had been called upon to fight and die at yet another distant place on the globe. This was in China, where American marines and infantrymen took part in a military relief expedition against the walled city of Tientsin and the so-called Forbidden City of Peking.

"Keep Up the Fire!"

While the United States was engaged in the war with Spain, several imperialistic European nations were busy in the Orient making efforts to divide and conquer China. The purpose of this division was for each nation to establish an exclusive "sphere of influence" in China where no other nation could carry on trade. The European nations involved in carving out these spheres of influence were Great Britain, Germany, Russia and France. Japan was also aggressively involved in the foreign efforts to dismember China.

As American ambassador to England, John Hay had been very much aware of European and Japanese imperialistic activities in the Far East. Since the United States had also long had a vital interest in the Orient, Hay was fearful that, during the Spanish-American War, China would be dismembered by

117

foreign powers and the United States cut off from all trade there. When the United States annexed the Philippines, America's vital interests in the Far East in general and China in particular were greatly increased.

In September 1899, after he had become U.S. secretary of state, Hay wrote a letter to the foreign powers involved in China, formally proposing what he called an "Open Door" policy there. This policy would not only guarantee China's continued existence as a nation, but it would also equalize the opportunity for all nations—and most especially the United States—to trade with China. Britain and Germany readily agreed, but the other nations were vague in their answers. Nevertheless, Hay proceeded on the basis that the Open Door was established policy, and the United States increased the size of its government staff at Peking.

The only problem was that China itself did not go along with either the Open Door policy or the spheres-of-influence plan. Many Chinese had grown angry at the ruthless exploitation of their country by foreign nations and were eager to bring this exploitation to an end. Thus they responded enthusiastically to the preachings of a secret society whose fanatical members wanted to drive out the "foreign devils." These violent Chinese nationalists were called Boxers, from the name of their society which was The Righteous Harmony Fists. Their insignia was the clenched fist, and their mystic belief was that faithful members of the society were immune to bullets—a belief similar to that of certain American Indians in their wars against the white man.

Encouraged by China's dowager empress, Tz'u Hsi, the Boxers began systematically killing foreigners in the spring of 1900. On June 20 the German ambassador was killed in Peking, creating a crisis situation. All other foreign civilians then took refuge in the international government or legation compound, where they were temporarily protected by military garrisons of the various foreign powers. This multinational military force, however, numbered only 445 men, including 55 U.S. Marines. Almost immediately they were besieged by thousands of Chinese, including not only Boxers but also Chinese regular army troops. Before the telegraph lines were cut, requests for help went out to Europe, Japan and the United States. The nations involved immediately began to form a military relief expedition.

Despite the fact that it was heavily engaged in the continued Philippine fighting, the United States made a large troop contribution to the international force. In addition, Manila was named the main staging base for the operation against China and the Boxers.

Following orders from Washington, General Mac-Arthur alerted the Ninth Infantry Regiment and a battalion of marines. They sailed from Manila and landed at Taku, a port near Tientsin and Peking, at the end of June. Soon they were joined by General Adna R. Chaffee, commander of the U.S. force, and a contingent of reinforcements that brought the U.S. troop total up to 2,500 men.

The international force of 6,000 men attacked Tientsin on July 13. Tientsin was a walled city that served as a protective barrier to Peking, about 75 miles away. The ensuing battle lasted 15 hours. When it was over, much of the fabled walled city lay in ruins, but the international force had defeated the Boxers, and the road to Peking lay open ahead.

There were many heroes at the Battle of Tientsin, but perhaps the most outstanding was Colonel Emerson H. Liscum, commanding officer of the U.S. Ninth Infantry. Tientsin was protected by two high walls, one of mud and the other of stone. When the allies moved up to attack at dawn on July 13, the outer mud wall had been breached by preliminary artillery fire. The Ninth Infantry, led by Colonel Liscum, was among the first units through the breached wall. As they moved into the city, they were immediately caught by severe enfilading or cross fire. One of the first men to go down was the Ninth's color-bearer, Sergeant John Gorman. As Sergeant Gorman fell, Colonel Liscum seized the colors and continued to move forward. Moments later, Liscum, too, was mortally wounded. Before he fell, however, he shouted to his steadily advancing troops, "Keep up the fire!" The Ninth kept up the fire and was instrumental in the fall of Tientsin and the later fall of Peking. Today, Liscum's battle cry is still the slogan of the Ninth Infantry, which serves behind the Demilitarized Zone in Korea. In honor of their China service, members of the Ninth are nicknamed The Manchus.

After consolidating their gains at Tientsin and receiving additional reinforcements, the allies marched on Peking early in August. The allied force now numbered about 18,000 men. They reached the gates of Peking on August 12, having fought several severe skirmishes along the way. On August 14, Peking's Outer City was captured, two U.S. infantry companies scaling the so-called Tartar Wall and furnishing covering fire to a British brigade that was the first to enter Peking. On the fifteenth, the Inner or Forbidden City was captured, the way being paved by extremely accurate American artillery fire from a unit called Reilly's Battery.

Entry into the Forbidden City saved the civilians who had taken refuge in the government legation buildings there. Military operations almost immediately came to an end, and an international army of occupation was set up.

Soon after the defeat of the Boxers at both Tientsin and Peking, China's dowager empress sued for peace, offering to resume all former trade agreements with the United States and other foreign powers. Her only request was the withdrawal of all foreign troops.

Negotiations, however, continued for months. All of the powers demanded severe reparation payments, including the United States, which demanded $25 million. But only half of this amount was ever actually received by the American government, and when

China paid that sum the United States insisted that it be used to educate Chinese students in the United States and for other educational work in China itself.

All of the foreign powers agreed to remove their troops by the fall of 1901. All of them did so except Russia, which maintained a large force in Manchuria. It was Japan's suspicions of Russia's intentions in China that would eventually lead to the Russo-Japanese War in 1904.

Some of the members of the American force that fought against the Boxers in China were returned to the United States when the Boxer Rebellion ended. Some of them remained in China for some months in the army of occupation. Many of them, however, were volunteers who reenlisted and returned to the Philippines, where they aided in the capture of Aguinaldo and the final defeat of the last of the *insurrecto* guerrilla bands who fought on after Aguinaldo had been captured.

After Aguinaldo's capture, guerrilla warfare continued for another year. By then more than 5,000 Americans and more than 20,000 Filipinos had been killed or had died of wounds or disease. American casualties in the Philippines and China—the latter accounting for another several hundred dead and wounded—outnumbered those suffered during the Spanish-American War itself.

It wasn't, in fact, until July 4, 1902, that the Philippine Insurrection officially came to an end—and it was ended then only by an official proclamation signed by the new president of the United States. Fittingly, that president was the man who had done so much to prepare the nation for the Spanish-American War, which had in turn led to America's new role as a world power. The new president was the old Rough Rider, Theodore Roosevelt.

Cowboy in the White House

Theodore Roosevelt had immediately gone back into politics when he returned from Cuba and resigned his army commission in 1898. The first office he sought was that of governor of New York on the Republican ticket. As a result of the Spanish-American War, Roosevelt was now a national hero. In his campaign he emphasized his Rough Rider role by taking with him the former bugler in the Rough Riders, who blew the cavalry charge call before each speech. In November, at the age of forty, Roosevelt was elected governor.

The New York State Republican boss was Senator Thomas C. Platt, who insisted that the new governor base his administration on political patronage and the spoils system (by giving out jobs on the basis of political party membership rather than merit). Roosevelt refused to do so. He played no party favorites and insisted that his administration be free of graft. Partly because of Platt's desire to "kick him upstairs" into a job where his reform measures could not damage the New York political machine, Roosevelt was suggested as the Republican vice-presidential candidate under McKinley in 1900. But McKinley was not eager to have Roosevelt as his running mate, fearing the headstrong Roosevelt might do more harm than good in stirring up foreign-policy problems.

McKinley, however, was facing a tough opponent in his bid for reelection. This was William Jennings Bryan, who had strongly opposed not only the annexation of the Philippines by the United States in 1898 but also America's continued military presence there. It was Bryan's opposition and that of the Democratic party that had almost defeated the Senate's ratification of the Treaty of Paris in February 1899. Supported by an organization called the Anti-Imperialist League, the Democrats were flatly opposed to the United States becoming a world power, if to do so meant annexing lands outside the continental United States. The United States, they said, had opposed imperialism ever since the days of the Monroe Doctrine in 1823.

McKinley had not easily become an imperialist. In fact, when it came to deciding in favor of the United States taking over Guam, Porto Rico and the Philippines from Spain, McKinley had, in his own words, "walked the floor of the White House night after night until midnight." Finally, he had "gone down on his

President William McKinley.

PHOTO: U.S. SIGNAL CORPS.

knees and prayed to Almighty God for light and guidance." Eventually he had decided that annexation was the only justifiable course of action.

Roosevelt, of course, had no such qualms. He saw America's expansion as the natural order of events. He *wanted* the United States to become a world power and, if annexation was the only way that goal could be reached, then so be it. "The question is not whether we should expand," he said, "for we have already expanded. The question is should we contract?" Most Americans agreed with Roosevelt's expansion ideas.

Thus it was that the old Rough Rider made a perfect running mate for McKinley in his bid for reelection in 1900, and McKinley was an astute enough politician to recognize the fact. He agreed that Roosevelt should be the Republican vice-presidential candidate.

The campaign proved to be a bitter one. Bryan and Edward Atkinson, leader of the Anti-Imperialist League, were vicious if not treasonable in their attacks on McKinley and Roosevelt. Among other things, they clearly "gave aid and comfort to the enemy" by urging American troops in the Philippines, fighting against Aguinaldo and his *insurrectos,* to refuse to continue fighting and "insist upon immediate discharge."

One Anti-Imperialist leaflet read: "We demand the immediate cessation of the war against liberty, begun by Spain and continued by us. We propose to contribute to the defeat of any person or party that stands for the forcible subjugation of any people."

Roosevelt and Rough Riders during mounted cavalry drill.

Before the U.S. national election of 1900, Aguinaldo and his followers had taken heart from such statements, all of which were passed on to them. But when the election actually took place, the Republican victory was a sweeping one. The American people obviously favored the true course of imperialism.

Roosevelt was greatly disappointed at being elected vice-president. "I'm through as a political figure," he said. "The Vice President never does anything that amounts to much."

Roosevelt presided over exactly one session of the Senate in 1901. On September 14, McKinley died as the result of a bullet fired by assassin Leon Czolgosz, and Roosevelt became the twenty-sixth president of the United States—at the age of forty-two, the youngest man ever to serve as president. (John F. Kennedy, at forty-three, was the youngest man ever to be elected president.)

"Now look," one of Roosevelt's political opponents said, "that damned cowboy has taken over the White House."

Take over the White House he did indeed and much else besides. Roosevelt never made any apologies for his imperialistic beliefs, although he never referred to them as being imperialistic. In 1903, for example, he was instrumental in getting Panama to secede from Colombia and form a separate republic so that the United States could obtain rights to build the Panama Canal from the "independent" Republic of Panama.

Officers of the Rough Riders.

One of Roosevelt's sayings was, "Walk softly, and carry a big stick." In 1905, he wielded his "big stick" by sending the U.S. Navy on a flag-showing world cruise, for which he was severely criticized by some people. But the president insisted he had sent "the great white fleet" on its cruise to insure world peace.

Also in 1905, the United States gained additional prestige as a world power when Roosevelt negotiated the end of the Russo-Japanese War in sessions at Portsmouth, New Hampshire. For these efforts he was later awarded the Nobel Peace Prize of $40,000. He used the money to establish a trust fund to promote industrial goodwill. During World War I, however, he dissolved the trust, and the money was used for war relief.

The old Rough Rider died quietly in his sleep on January 6, 1919, at Sagamore Hill. He was buried in a cemetery nearby. For good or ill, the results of the Spanish-American War—"my war," as he often called it—have lived on after him right up to the present day.

Bibliography

Bassett, John Spencer, *Makers of a New Nation* (*The Pageant of America,* Vol. IX), Yale University Press, New Haven, Conn., 1928

Berky, Andrew S., and Shenton, James P., editors, *The Historians' History of the United States,* G. P. Putnam's Sons, New York, 1966

Bishop, Joseph Bucklin, *Theodore Roosevelt and His Time,* Charles Scribner's Sons, New York, 1920

Esposito, Colonel Vincent J., *The West Point Atlas of American Wars,* Frederick Praeger Publishers, New York, 1959

Fish, Carl Russel, and Seymour, Charles, *The Rise to World Power* (*The Chronicles of America,* Vol. 23), Yale University Press, New Haven, Conn., 1919

Freidel, Frank, *The Splendid Little War,* Little, Brown and Co., Boston, 1958

Gurney, Gene, *A Pictorial History of the United States Army,* Crown Publishers, New York, 1966

Johnson, Thomas H., *The Oxford Companion to American*

History, Oxford University Press, New York, 1966

Leckie, Robert, *The Wars of America,* Harper and Row, New York, 1968

Lorant, Stefan, *The Life and Times of Theodore Roosevelt,* Doubleday & Co., Garden City, New York, 1959

Morison, Samuel Eliot, *The Oxford History of the American People,* Oxford University Press, New York, 1965

Roberts, W. Adolphe, and Brentano, Lowell, editors, *The Book of the Navy* (anthology), Doubleday, Doran & Co., Garden City, New York, 1944

Roosevelt, Theodore, *The Rough Riders,* Charles Scribner's Sons, New York, 1920

Roosevelt, Theodore, *An Autobiography,* The Macmillan Co., New York, 1913

Steele, Matthew Forney, *American Campaigns,* War Department, Document No. 324, Washington, D.C., 1909

Swanberg, W. A., *Citizen Hearst,* Charles Scribner's Sons, New York, 1961

Taylor, Charles Carlisle, *The Life of Admiral Mahan,* George H. Doran Co., New York, 1920

U.S. Army, ROTC Manual No. 145-20, *American Military History, 1607–1958,* Department of the Army, U.S. Government Printing Office, Washington, D.C., 1959

Weigley, Russell, *The American Way of War,* Macmillan, New York, 1972

Wood, William, and Gabriel, Ralph Henry, *In Defense of Liberty* (*The Pageant of America,* Vol. VII), Yale University Press, New Haven, Conn., 1928

Index

137